Things We Don't Talk About

Help for the Private Struggles of Ordinary Adventists

SKIP MacCarty

REVIEW AND HERALD® PUBLISHING ASSOCIATION
HAGERSTOWN, MD 21740

Unless otherwise noted, Bible texts in this book are from the *Holy Bible, New International Version.* Copyright © 1973, 1978, 1984, International Bible Society. Used by permission of Zondervan Bible Publishers.

Texts credited to KJV are from the King James Version.

Scripture quotations marked NASB are from the *New American Standard Bible,* © The Lockman Foundation 1960, 1962, 1963, 1968, 1971, 1972, 1973, 1975, 1977.

Texts credited to NKJV are from The New King James Version. Copyright © 1979, 1980, 1982, Thomas Nelson, Inc., Publishers.

Bible texts credited to NRSV are from the New Revised Standard Version of the Bible, copyright © 1989 by the Division of Christian Education of the National Council of the Churches of Christ in the U.S.A. Used by permission.

Bible texts credited to Phillips are from J. B. Phillips: *The New Testament in Modern English,* Revised Edition. © J. B. Phillips 1958, 1960, 1972. Used by permission of Macmillan Publishing Co.

Bible texts credited to RSV are from the Revised Standard Version of the Bible, copyright © 1946, 1952, 1971, by the Division of Christian Education of the National Council of the Churches of Christ in the U.S.A. Used by permission.

Bible texts credited to TEV are from the *Good News Bible*—Old Testament: Copyright © American Bible Society 1976; New Testament: Copyright © American Bible Society 1966, 1971, 1976.

Verses marked TLB are taken from *The Living Bible,* copyright © 1971 by Tyndale House Publishers, Wheaton, Ill. Used by permission.

This book was
Edited by Gerald Wheeler
Designed by Patricia S. Wegh
Cover photo by Tony Stone Images
Interior photos by Joel D. Springer
Typeset: Times 12.5/13.5

PRINTED IN U.S.A.

01 00 99 98 97   10 9 8 7 6 5 4 3 2 1

R&H Cataloging Service
MacCarty, William Arthur (Skip), 1943-
    Things we don't talk about: help for the private struggles
of ordinary Adventists.
    1. Religious life. 2. Seventh-day Adventists–Religious
life. I. Title.

286.732

ISBN 0-8280-1093-5

PREFACE

When I asked a friend to read the first few chapters of this book in manuscript form, he glanced at the title and sneered amicably, "Oh, come on now, do you really believe there's such a thing in the 1990s as an ordinary Adventist?" Little did he know how that very question had inflicted me with writing paralysis more than a year and a half earlier.

It was the summer of 1990 when Penny Wheeler, then acquisitions editor for Review and Herald® Publishing Association, first suggested that I write on this subject. While she was a guest lecturer at a writers' conference I was attending at Andrews University, we had lunch together and discussed the unique challenges Seventh-day Adventists experience in attempting to live a successful, vibrant Christian life. Between mouthfuls of mock chicken nuggets, mashed potatoes, and a small garden salad (staple fare, as I later mused, for ordinary Seventh-day Adventists), I disclosed my own personal struggles in Christian living from my earliest upbringing as an Adventist. I had noted similar inner conflicts in other Seventh-day Adventists who had confided in me through the years. And through the years I had also discovered some powerful spiritual principles that had helped me greatly.

Minutes before Penny had to rush to her next presentation, I caught a daring gleam in her eye. "Why don't you write on this subject?" she challenged. "We could call it *The Private Life of an Ordinary Adventist.*" I smiled politely and nodded, implying that her suggestion intrigued me. In reality it scared me to death. *Come on, Penny,* I thought, *do you really think there's such a thing today as an ordinary Adventist?* Eighteen months later she was still assuring me that it would be a very valuable book for Seventh-day Adventists.

A Common Struggle With Diversity

During that 18-month interim I had been thinking, praying, and agonizing about Penny's invitation. It occurred to me that the Seventh-day Adventist Church today is marbled with a rich diversity that is both promising and disturbing. An analysis of many Adventist congregations might reveal a mix as varied as the following:

- members who are liberal in both theology and lifestyle, and others who are conservative in both;
- members who are theologically liberal but conservative in lifestyle, and vice versa;
- members who cooperate with the church program, and others who pull against it;
- members who regularly invest time and money in the church, and others who seldom support it;
- members who are financially prospering, and others who are barely surviving;
- members who have doctoral degrees, and others who haven't graduated from high school;
- members who are noted professionals in the community, and others on welfare;
- members who are happily married, and others who live with chronic marital tension or are painfully divorced;
- members who eat meat, and others who won't even touch eggs or drink milk;
- members who suspect that certain members of their church are not true Christians, and others who suspect the same about *them.*

Living in a climate of differing viewpoints on either end of the spectrum is part of what it means to be an ordinary Adventist today. Whether we like it or not, members with perhaps unprecedented differences of viewpoint and lifestyle worship side by side in our pews. That may not be quite as noticeable in Berrien Springs, Michigan, as it is in Provo, Utah, or in Winnemucca, Nevada. Having pastored over the years in the latter two communities, among others, I have been struck with one notable dissimilarity. Berrien Springs has 11 Adventist churches within 15 miles of my home. Two of the congregations believe the Bible prohibits the ordination of women as local elders, while in two others women presently serve as first elders. When an Adventist moves to Berrien Springs, he or she simply finds the local Adventist church with the most compatible beliefs and joins it. However, an Adventist moving to Provo, Utah, or to Winnemucca, Nevada, doesn't have that same luxury. It's too far to drive to the next nearest Adventist church. In such communities members with differing theological viewpoints and Christian lifestyles worship side by side, sometimes uncomfortably. Such diversity is one of those unspoken things we hesitate to talk about.

Some Common Threads

But belonging to a diverse community is only one of the unmentioned spiritual struggles ordinary Adventists encounter. Over the years I have related to hundreds of Adventists of vastly different backgrounds, careers, educational achievements, economic levels, social attainments, lifestyle choices, and personal viewpoints. And yet as dissimilar as we are in many ways, many of us have remarkably similar struggles of the heart that, while complex and deeply personal, weave their way like common threads through our daily experiences as Christians. These common threads—the common heart struggles of Christian living, the things we would like to share and discuss with each other but are often afraid to—make up the theme of this book.

Ordinary Adventists have times when they feel secure with God. They know the incomparable joy of the assurance of salvation, of feeling ready to meet Jesus should their life end at that very moment. By and large they long for Jesus to come. But they also experience other times when they feel so defeated in their spiritual walk that it seems as though eternal salvation is nothing but a false hope for them. Perhaps they may even wonder if they have ever really been converted, or if it's all been an illusion. Sometimes they are actually afraid for Jesus to come. While they know they're not supposed to react that way, they still do. And they feel uncomfortable talking about it. If you ever feel like this, you're an ordinary Adventist.

Ordinary Adventists have experienced moments of devotional-time ecstasy. They've gotten up early and spent significant time with God in Bible study and prayer, sensed God's presence, and seen their prayers answered right before their eyes. But they've had other times when they came away from attempted communication with God feeling empty. It was as though the well had run dry. Their devotional study seemed boring and unproductive and their prayers didn't seem to make a difference anymore. It even hurt to pray, because it seemed to raise false hopes. And they knew this wasn't God's fault. But neither did they know what had gone wrong. Sometimes the dry spells were prolonged and led to discouragement or abandonment of the daily devotional life. If you've ever experienced this, you're an ordinary Adventist.

Ordinary Adventists want their family to be harmonious and happy. They believe, "With Jesus in the family, happy, happy home." So they pray for Him to be part of their family. But sometimes theirs isn't a happy, happy home. And that's extremely hard to relate to. They hope other church members don't find out that they have family problems. Recognizing that their family is their first responsibility, if it's not always a happy, happy home, they wonder what it says about them as Christians. Yet they're too embarrassed to ask for help. They feel prayer alone should solve such problems. And sometimes it does. *Sometimes.*

Ordinary Adventists have had experiences in the church that hurt, and that made it hard for them to keep going back. They have a hard time knowing how to relate to other members who seem to believe differently, and live by different standards, than they do. At times they are enthusiastically active in the church, and other times the fire just seems to go out of their involvement, and they aren't sure what to do to rekindle it. Sometimes they're confused about how to know God's will. Other times it seems as if they're losing ground spiritually, even though they may be trying harder than ever. Caught up in their busy schedules, they don't think much about the final crisis, but when they do, they're not sure they're ready for it. What the bottom line of the spiritual life is all about troubles them occasionally. Embarrassing and unsuccessful attempts in the past have made them leery about witnessing.

If you can relate to any of these experiences, you're an ordinary Adventist struggling with those things we hesitate to talk about.

I've found that many ordinary Adventists believe that they are the only ones who experience spiritual ups and downs. It often seems to them as though everyone else is doing just fine. That sense of spiritual loneliness and isolation is one of the reasons it's so hard at times being an ordinary Adventist.

I'm One Too

Upon serious reflection, I've come to the humbling conclusion that despite being an ordained minister, I'm also a quite ordinary Adventist when it comes to the challenges of successfully living the Christian life day by day. Reared in an Adventist family, educated in Adventist schools from the first grade through my Doctor of Ministry degree, I have breathed Adventist subculture all my life. In some respects that makes me different from many Adventists who converted to the Adventist faith later in life, a difference accentuated further by my career as a minister. But different in these respects does not necessarily mean unordinary, especially in the daily attempt to live successfully as an Adventist Christian.

Some of my most memorable spiritual experiences have grown out of periods of my most intense spiritual conflicts as an ordinary Adventist dealing with unspoken issues. Great problems can lead to great progress, deep spiritual conflict to even deeper spiritual conversion. The down times can be as significant as the up times, the dry times as fertile as the ecstatic times, in terms of what God can build into our lives. That makes life as an ordinary Adventist today a challenging, unpredictable, exciting adventure.

How to Read

I've written this book with a certain progression in mind. First I concentrate on some of the too-little-discussed challenges we Adventists encounter in our efforts to relate to God in a personal way (the "Looking to Him" section). Then in the "Looking at One Another" section I try to be quite open about what happens in our relationships to one another as Adventists. Next I turn to the interior struggle, the "Looking Within" perspective, our deep inner questing for spiritual authenticity and integrity. "Looking Out at the World" focuses on some of the challenges we face in personally participating in the Adventist mission. And finally, "Looking Through His Eyes" conjectures a divine perspective on us ordinary Adventists, a perspective that we're given permission, if not invited, to share.

Hopefully you will find a measure of cumulative value in reading the entire book through in the order written. However, it may be even more valuable for some readers to pick and choose those chapters that address issues that particularly interest them or that relate to a particular aspect of the Adventist experience that they may be struggling with at the moment. Each chapter was written with that possibility in mind.

Thank You!

This book in its present form is largely the result of several very significant people in my life. My friend and colleague, Dwight K. Nelson, senior pastor of the Pioneer Memorial church at Andrews University, both encouraged and bore long with me, a junior member of his staff, as I wrote. My good neighbor Buddy Shepherd in a labor of love kept up my yard during the summer I finished this book and prepared to accompany Pastor Nelson on an evangelistic trip to India. Discussions with our oldest son, Michael, have kept me honestly working on the intellectual moorings of my faith. Pam, one of our twins, suggested including the chapter on God's will. Madeline Johnston gave invaluable editorial assistance for the first several chapters before she left for an extended trip to Israel. Chuck and Barbara Randall graciously provided a retreat center in their home during a critical time of the writing. Barbara was God's special gift as she spent many hours helping me say the same thing in fewer words.

I dedicate this book to my author-widowed wife, Lyn, who for many months of Sundays, holidays, and some vacation days, patiently allowed me to squirrel myself away at the computer. Her love and support, and the insights I've gained from her, have made this book in a good measure what it is. I love you, sweetheart.

LOOKING TO HIM

confusion GUILT FEAR doubt

CHAPTER ONE

The Flips and Flops of the Ordinary Adventist's Assurance of Salvation

When my three sons were considerably younger, the four of us were playing the Ungame together one afternoon. One of the cards frequently drawn in this relationship-building game enables the cardholder to ask any question he or she wishes of any player in the group. Over the course of the game I got the three cards I wanted and asked each of my sons what he would want if he could be guaranteed any one thing in life. All three gave the same answer: To go to heaven with Jesus when He returns.

A purist might have criticized them for not asking for wisdom, as Solomon did. But I was proud of them for not demanding a lifetime supply of Reese's Pieces. Their answer highlighted a deep-seated desire of all Christians—to be assured of salvation.

As a young boy growing up in the Adventist Church, I vividly remember how I longed to be ready for Jesus to come. But I honestly felt that I would never make it. Down the pew from me in church each Sabbath sat Brother William Miller (no relation to the nineteenth-century Baptist revivalist whose prophetic preaching sparked the Adventist movement). Brother Miller was a real saint and revered by everyone in our congregation. He never wiggled in church or did anything else wrong that I ever heard of. I knew he would make it. But me? I kept getting into a heap of trouble for wiggling and whispering in church, and for doing things wrong at home, too. I felt I'd never be good enough to make it.

Another thing I envied about Brother Miller was the fact that he was old and didn't have to be good very much longer. *If I were as old as Brother Miller,* I thought, *maybe I could be good long enough to make it.* But I was sure that I couldn't be good for all the years ahead of me. I felt as if getting to heaven was an impossible dream.

Now I can smile at the immaturity of some of the conclusions that seemed so logical then. But deep into my adult years the feelings of insecurity with God persisted as an insidious parasite, robbing me of the spontaneous joy and praise that comes when we finally experience true assurance.

Roller-coaster Experience

I remember the first time that I really felt I could be saved. A class at the Andrews University Theological Seminary made the writings of Paul come alive and powerfully impact my life. Lecture by lecture, Hans K. LaRondelle intellectually dismantled the legalistic edifice of my spiritual formation and introduced me to a righteousness from God that was already mine through faith in Jesus Christ. It wasn't that I had never heard such teachings before. But somehow it came to me as something wonderfully new.

I remember the day that it finally sank home, and I began to really believe I could be saved—I mean, really *believe and feel* that I had salvation. I went back to my apartment that day and began praising God spontaneously. Then to celebrate, I ate a whole pan of fudge brownies! You could appreciate that only if you had grown up believing that such intemperate indulgence was a near mortal sin.

I wish I could say that from that time on I have always felt sure of my salvation. The truth is, however, it's been a roller-coaster experience for most of my life—sometimes feeling sure I could be saved, at other times struggling with insecurity. And I've since discovered that my experience is not unique.

One former member in Winnemucca, Nevada, told me, "I know I can never be saved, so why even try?" Another member who attended regularly told me that he didn't expect to be saved because he knew he had too many faults. At first I thought he was kidding and tried to joke with him about it. But as our conversation continued, I realized he was serious. Then I began to feel sorry for him. Finally I remembered how I too felt the riptides of spiritual insecurity surging through my own heart.

The assurance of salvation comes hard for many of us ordinary Adventists.

The Root of the Problem

Some Adventists seem to have a constant sense of security with God. A good friend of mine, a vibrant Christian for whom I have the highest respect, once told me that when he heard that only one out of 20 church members were ready for Jesus to come, he instinctively felt sorry for the other 19 in his group. At the opposite end of the spectrum are those who feel they don't have a chance. Some drop out of the church, while others seem almost addicted to church and can't stop going even though they've lost all hope. Most of us ordinary Adventists camp somewhere between the two extremes, or perhaps oscillate between them. Why?

Some of our critics claim that something inherent in the Adventist doctrine breeds spiritual insecurity. We would say that the Adventist message is the most beautiful and assuring word God has ever given. But then why don't we experience a more constant sense of security in our relationship with God?

It's important to realize that Adventists are not the only ones who struggle with this. A friend of mine, Markus Hill, a psychologist who spent most of his adult life worshiping, even pastoring for a few years, in non-Adventist congregations, read an early draft of this manuscript and remarked, "You're not just dealing with an Adventist problem here. It is a problem for Christians in general."

Of course it is. The problem of insecurity with God isn't rooted in some faulty point of Adventist doctrine—it lies in the sinful nature of man! We were born estranged from God, and it's Satan's studied effort not only to keep us from reconciling with God, but to keep us constantly unsure of His love and acceptance.

A Misplaced Focus

After I ate the pan of fudge brownies to celebrate my newly discovered security of salvation, I wrote a sermon to tell people that they could know they were saved. I started with the question "Have you come to where, in your Christian experience, you honestly believe you are saved and can say 'I am saved'?" I based the sermon on the Bible's classic passage on the assurance of salvation, 1 John 5:13: "I write these things to you who believe in the name of the Son of God so that you may know that you have eternal life." My sermon implied that Adventists were immature Christians if they couldn't with absolute confidence say "I am saved," as I now felt I could.

But as I continued studying on this subject, I wasn't able to find a single instance in which a biblical prophet or apostle ever said "I am saved." That doesn't mean they didn't feel secure in their relationship with God. But their messages have a different focus. As I continued to explore the subject, I even found that 1 John 5:13, in context, teaches that the assurance of salvation comes to those who focus not on such assurance as an end in itself, but on God's love for us and, in response, on our love for Him and others as expressed in obedience and service.

The assurance of salvation is like happiness, alluding those who pursue it as an end in itself, but found by those who seek other worthwhile pursuits in life. It's a result, not a goal. Jesus said that eternal life itself comes not from searching for it as an end in itself, but from seeking God (John 17:3). The same is true of the assurance of salvation.

Eventually I retired my sermons on the assurance of salvation. If I was convinced that preaching on the assurance of salvation would really help people obtain it, I would still do it. But I have become convinced that in fact the opposite is true.

I did find one group in the Bible who spoke very confidently about their salvation. They boasted, "We are Abraham's descendants," while they plotted to kill Jesus (John 8:33, 37). In the Sermon on the Mount Jesus warned that some who feel very sure about their salvation will one day hear Him say: "I never knew you. Away from me, you evildoers" (Matt. 7:21-23).

Jesus Himself didn't go around claiming "I am saved." Nor did He ask anyone else, "Do you know that you are saved? Can you say that you are saved?" He focused on His Father's love and went about demonstrating that love to others (John 3:16, 34, 35; 10:17; etc.).

Finding It but Losing It

Jesus said, "Whoever wants to save his life will lose it, but whoever loses his life for me will find it" (Matt. 16:25). I can testify from my own experience that when I sought for the assurance of salvation, I didn't attain it in any lasting way. Let me tell you the excruciating story of how I eventually found it by losing it.

I experienced a time when many personal problems converged and overwhelmed me. Within an hour after waking in the morning I would be exhausted from the sheer weight of the problems. It was all I could do to drag myself to my office for a few hours. I felt like a terrible hypocrite counseling others when my own life was in such a shambles. Constantly I felt like a totally lost man, with no hope at all.

One night my despair became unbearable, and I staggered around the square of an open shopping mall, groping for even one reason to keep trying. A policeman concluded that he had a drunk on his hands, but he finally accepted my explanation of needing time to think and pray.

Lying down on a bench, after an indeterminate period of simply gazing at the sky, I told God that I knew I was a lost man. At that moment I experienced the complete opposite of the assurance of salvation—I felt sure I could never be saved.

That was my personal Gethsemane. Ellen White says that as Jesus hung on the cross, He couldn't see past the portals of the tomb.[1] He endured what the lost will feel at the moment of second death. Jesus felt not just a little unsure of His salvation, but totally lost! And that night at the mall I couldn't see past that bench I was lying on. My hope had been completely crushed out, not magnanimously or heroically by the sins of others as Jesus experienced, but by the sense of my own selfishness, sinfulness, and failures.

I wrestled with God the rest of that night, not over my salvation anymore, but over what to do with my life as a lost man. I knew it didn't matter anymore what I did, as far as my salvation was concerned. I couldn't get any more lost than I already was. If there were things I hadn't done just because I thought I might be doomed for doing them, they were all possible now.

Out of the hellish agony of that night's experience I made an incredible discovery—whether I would be saved in the end or not, all I wanted was to live for God and to bring Him glory, even if that meant that God would show the world through my life the tragic results of being lost, so that it could warn others and thus perhaps save someone. Once I confessed that to God, I sensed Him answering me, not with an audible voice, but nevertheless clearly, that with that decision made I could leave all matters pertaining to my personal salvation to Him.

Thus my intense struggle ended. I returned to my apartment and slept peacefully. Ironically, I still didn't feel that I would be saved. But that didn't really matter right then, because I had already resigned myself to being lost. It was several days later, as I remember, before I began to have hope again for my personal salvation. But it was different from before. This time I wasn't searching for it. This time I was seeking to glorify God and help others, and the assurance came as a by-product. Nor was it so much a confidence of salvation as it was a sense of His love for me and a knowledge that I could safely trust Him with my future no matter what.

Several months after my experience at the mall I was intrigued to learn that the great Christian John Bunyan himself had severe bouts with spiritual insecurity for the majority of his Christian life. In his autobiography, *Grace Abounding to the Chief of Sinners,* Bunyan relates that he felt that he might even have committed the unpardonable sin. One day he came across 2 Corinthians 12:9: "My grace is sufficient for thee" (KJV) and found that its promise could overcome the doubts that assailed him. Yet, when imprisoned for his preaching, he again fell into despair that he had never truly been accepted by God. Finally he defeated the tempter's assault upon his security with God when he vowed to go on with Christ whether he be finally saved or not. And John Bunyan then gave the world *The Pilgrim's Progress.*

I found my experience further confirmed in *Steps to Christ:* "We should not make self the center and indulge anxiety and fear as to whether we shall be saved. All this turns the soul away from the Source of our strength. Commit the keeping of your soul to God, and trust in Him. . . . Rest in God. He is able to keep that which you have committed to Him. If you will leave yourself in His hands, He will bring you off more than conqueror through Him that has loved you" (p. 72).

"Oh, Daddy"

When my three sons were young we would go on backpacking trips together each summer into the wilderness area of Utah's Uinta Mountains. On one trip Marcus, my youngest son, and I were sleeping in one tent, while Michael, my oldest, and his brother Andrew were in their own tent about 20 yards away. During the middle of our first night out, I was startled awake by a blood-curdling scream.

I recognized Andrew's voice. With visions of carnivorous preda-
tors racing through my mind, I grabbed my flashlight, unzipped our
tent, and shined the light on the other tent. Sure enough, it was
moving. Racing over to their tent, I zipped it open and aimed my
light inside. The scene before me told the story.

Andrew had awakened to pitch blackness and didn't know
where he was. That was frightening enough, but then he sat up, causing his head to hit the tent, terrifying him. The look on his face was
one of such abject horror that it scared me even though I knew by
then that he was OK. Suddenly I realized that I was not helping matters by shining my light in his face, for that made him even more
frightened. So I quickly turned the beam back onto my own face.

The rest of the story occurred faster than it takes me to type this
sentence. The lines of fright and terror on his face melted into complete peace as he said, "Oh, Daddy." Within literally five seconds
of saying those words he had lain down and gone back to sleep. In
the morning he couldn't remember the incident. Nor could either of
his brothers. But it was a scene that I will never forget. His face
melting from fear into complete security after a split-second
glimpse of the face of his father whom he trusted and with whom
he was friends.

In the Sermon on the Mount, Jesus shone His light on the
Father's face, a face that can bring peace to every heart that beholds
it and learns to know its trustworthy love. He asked parents to re-
call when their own children were high-chair age and crying for
food. Could you imagine yourself, He inquired, scooping a pile of
rocks onto the high-chair tray to answer the hungry cry of your
baby? Even worse, could you envision yourself tossing a poisonous
snake onto the tray? Of course not! Even though we are selfish by
nature and limited as to what we can provide, we still protect and
care for our children. Then Jesus thrust home His all-important
point: Your heavenly Father will, to the fullest extent of His un-
conditional love and power, protect and care for you, His trusting
child (Matt. 7:9-11).

Some have expressed to me that picturing God as their Parent
makes them feel insecure and afraid because of the abuse they suffered at the hands of their human parents. But Jesus didn't ask us to
view God through the image of our parents, but rather to think of
Him as we would envision ourselves ideally relating to our own

children. I've had people tell me that the switch in viewpoints has freed them to see God in a whole new way.

"Christ's favorite theme was the paternal character and abundant love of God,"[2] Ellen White wrote. "There is nothing so great and powerful as God's love for those who are His children."[3] Accepting and experiencing the parental love God has for me has given me the greatest security I've ever experienced. For that reason Christ's favorite theme has become my own favorite.

Jesus showed the Father's face by the way He lived. He treated everyone He met with the same care and respect He would have wanted if He were in their place. We can be secure with Someone like that.

Jesus has set us free to focus on the Father and His love for us, free to seek His glory and the good of others. *He is our security.* Ordinary Adventists need only rest in God. He is able to guard that which we have entrusted to Him for that day (2 Tim. 1:12).

---

[1] Ellen G. White, *The Desire of Ages* (Mountain View, Calif.: Pacific Press Pub. Assn., 1898), p. 753.

[2] ———, *Testimonies for the Church* (Mountain View, Calif.: Pacific Press Pub. Assn., 1948), vol. 6, p. 55.

[3] ———, *Our Father Cares* (Hagerstown, Md.: Review and Herald Pub. Assn., 1991), p. 32.

CHAPTER TWO

How Good Do I Really Have to Be to Make It?

I'm hooked on football. Will that keep me out of heaven? I know that God loves me—I have no doubt whatsoever about that. And I don't worry so much as I used to about whether I will be saved. Resting in our Father's love has brought me great peace. But still, each fall I start feeling guilty again about the tenacious hold that football has on me. Even if I go shopping with Lyn on Sunday, I'm thinking about football. If we stop at Sears, she knows she can find me in the TV section keeping track of the scores. Is there anything really wrong with my enjoyment of football? Is that something I need to give up? And what will happen to me if I don't, as far as my relationship with God and heaven are concerned?

I'm not attempting to solve the football question in this chapter. Instead I'm just using football as an example. If another ordinary Adventist were writing this chapter, the more appropriate example might be overeating, or eating too many desserts, or going to the movies, or masturbation, or overspending, or watching R-rated videos, or playing video games by the hour, or wearing a pair of tiny stud earrings—the list could probably fill a book in itself. Do we need to overcome such kinds of things in order to be saved?

Eight times the book of Revelation emphasizes the importance of being an overcomer. Note some of the good things it says about it:

- "To him who overcomes, I will give the right to eat from the tree of life" (Rev. 2:7).
- "He who overcomes will not be hurt at all by the second death" (verse 11).
- "To him who overcomes, I will give some of the hidden manna" (verse 17).
- "To him who overcomes and does my will to the end, I will give authority over the nations" (verse 26).
- "He who overcomes will . . . be dressed in white. I will never blot out his name from the book of life" (Rev. 3:5).
- "To him who overcomes, I will give the right to sit with me on my throne" (verse 21).
- "He who overcomes will inherit all this, and I will be his God and he will be my son" (Rev. 21:7).

Read in their contexts, the passages are even stronger. They suggest that on the day Jesus gathers His children to inherit the kingdom He has prepared for them, all those who aren't overcomers will end up outside the Holy City looking in.

Tough Questions

Does that answer my question about whether I have to give up watching football to be saved? If I have an inner sense that football has become a real problem for me, do I then have to discard it to be an overcomer? Isn't it possible that I just have an overly sensitive conscience, and that I really don't have to abandon football after all? That's what many of my friends have told me, that I should relax and enjoy the diversion of a football game once in a while.

Doesn't the suggestion that I have to avoid football fall into the category of righteousness by works? How can turning my back on football save me? And when someone says "Giving up football won't save you, but not giving it up could cause you to be lost," isn't that really saying the same thing with different words?

I realize that some people try to rationalize everything, so that they can justify doing anything they want. Take the example cited by Leighton Ford: "Mickey Cohen, the Los Angeles racketeer, wanted to know why, if there were Christian politicians and Christian singers, he couldn't be a 'Christian gangster'! It was news to Mickey that Jesus didn't come to ratify his sins but to save him from them." *

But where should we draw the line as to what is sin and needs to be overcome?

We recently asked a member, whom I'll call Mary, to hold an important office in our church. Mary told me that even though she attended church each Sabbath, she wasn't sure how she felt about being an Adventist. Reared in a very strict environment, she once believed that it was a sin for a woman ever to wear slacks.

Is it possible that watching football for me could be compared to wearing slacks for Mary? Perhaps what I really need to overcome is a false sense of guilt.

Mary's upbringing made her fearful of God. Eventually she came in contact with a group of Adventists who held a very different view of God and the Adventist message. Feeling liberated by this new view, she discarded her previously held concepts of what constituted the Adventist lifestyle. Now she was adding back into her life only those things that she believed were clearly taught in the Bible. Mary told me that when she wasn't at church, she wore jewelry. She wondered if that would keep her from serving in the church office we were asking her to fill. I had to tell her that according to present church policy, as I understand it, she could not do both.

But would Mary have to discard jewelry to be an overcomer in the sense in which Revelation calls Christians to be overcomers? A perfectionistic viewpoint would undoubtedly render a ready affirmative—"Can we really be perfectly reflecting the character of Jesus while wearing jewelry?" A more liberal-minded approach would probably consider such a query as majoring in minors— "Shouldn't we really be focusing on salvation and love rather than on externals?" Many of our local churches contain both viewpoints.

In my file I have a paper written by an Adventist minister who attempts to defend the wearing of jewelry from a biblical perspective. It examines exegetically all the texts we have traditionally used to discourage the use of jewelry and concludes that at best the Bible does not condemn it. Another author, Martin Weber, in his book *Adventist Hot Potatoes* defends the wearing of the wedding band with arguments that one could just as easily apply to other forms of jewelry. The dialogue extends, intensely and uncomfortably at times, to many local congregations, as many ordinary Adventists well know.

As Adventist disciples of Jesus Christ, God calls us to be "in the world" but "not of the world" (John 17:13-16). That's at the heart of the dialogue, isn't it? To what extent do our standards remove us from a needed identification with the world that God has called us to be in and witness to? On the other hand, at what point does conformity to the world's lifestyle compromise the purity of the image of Jesus that it is our privilege to portray? He lived among us in such utter simplicity and freedom from the competitive and spellbinding entertainments that mesmerized the masses.

The question is, To what extent do any of the items on our list need to be overcome in order not to forfeit our right to inherit the eternal kingdom Jesus is preparing for us?

Reframing the Question

What makes this question so difficult is that no specific Bible texts mention football or many of the other What's-wrong-with-_____ ? items on our list. We must decide such issues based on principles rather than direct commands.

The Bible doesn't offer easy answers to the how-much-can-I-be-like-the-world-without-becoming-part-of-it types of questions. A different mentality altogether operates in the Bible. It's best illustrated by a story I once heard in a sermon as a boy.

Once upon a time (the best stories always seem to start like that) a rich baron lived in a big castle. The castle sat atop a very high and steep mountain. The road leading there from the valley below was narrow and treacherous.

The baron needed to hire a driver who could maneuver his horse-drawn coach back and forth down the mountain to the little town in the valley below. Safety was of utmost concern. To each of the three applicants he meticulously explained about the dangers of the rough and narrow road—carved out of sheer cliff in places—they would be traveling each day.

Eager to impress the baron, the first applicant extolled his skills, boasting that he could drive a coach within a foot of the edge and not lose it. "That's impressive indeed," the baron replied.

The second man then assured the nobleman that he was so adept at negotiating treacherous terrain that he could safely take the coach from the top of the mountain to the valley below with only six inches between the wheels of the coach and a plunge down the face of the mountain. "That's more impressive still," the baron said as he stroked his well-groomed beard.

"And you, sir," the baron asked the third man, "how close can you drive to the edge of the cliff and still be safe?"

"I don't know," the third man said rather humbly. "I always stay as far away from the edge as I possibly can." Whereupon he was hired.

That's the mental attitude that runs through the writings of the prophets. Not How much can I conform to the world and still not be lost? Not How close can I live to hell and still get to heaven? The question the prophets wrestle with is How close can I live to God so that my total life and influence reveal His purity and love?

Take, for example, how Paul related to the issue of eating food offered to idols (1 Cor. 8). That's a rather dead controversy today—the Adventist Church doesn't even take an official position on it. It's certainly not one of the subjects I'm struggling with in my life. But in Paul's day it was a hot potato.

The issue arose when pagans began to convert to Christianity. As pagans they would eat food that had been offered to idols. Farmers would take their food to the temple and have it ritually blessed before the pagan gods. Some would then mark up the price in the marketplace. Many pagans paid the higher prices to earn the good graces of the gods. On any given day, the best quality food available at the marketplace was very likely food that had been routinely presented to the gods.

When pagans became Christians, was it right for them to continue to eat food offered in ritual blessing to false gods? Paul reasoned that the "gods" of the pagans were not real gods at all, and thus the food offered to such nonexistent entities wasn't intrinsically evil (1 Cor. 8:4-6, 8). Thus technically, on the basis of this knowledge alone, he was free to eat it.

But he went on to say that that conclusion rested purely on rational argument, and for Christians there is something more determinative than logic alone—Christian love (verses 1-3). He reasoned that pagans, without his enlightened understanding on the subject, might see him eating such food, think he believed in their gods, and be emboldened in their pagan practices through his example. For that reason, he said, "I will never eat meat [offered to idols] again" (verse 13). Then he told the Corinthians that if they continued to consume food offered to idols, they would be setting an example that would lead unenlightened and weak-conscienced individuals deeper into sin (verse 11). And if that wasn't strong enough, he added: "When you sin against your brothers in this way and wound their weak conscience, you sin against Christ" (verse 12).

To summarize: Paul began with the question the Corinthians were debating, Can I eat food offered to idols and be saved? After initially answering that there was nothing intrinsically wrong with such food, Paul shifted the focus to what he considered the even more important question: Will eating such food enable me to be the best possible influence for Jesus to those He has called me to serve? The latter is a very different question from the former. First Corinthians 10:31 states it in the form of a principle: "Whether you eat or drink or whatever you do, do it all for the glory of God."

The B.C. and A.D. Questions

We could consider these the B.C. and A.D. questions. We all know that B.C. dates events before Christ, and A.D., after Christ (literally, Latin *anno Domini,* "in the year of our Lord"). The coming of Jesus into the world split history in two, into the B.C. and A.D. eras. Similarly, the entry of Jesus into our personal lives divides them into two distinct periods. In the B.C. period of life the essential question is "What must I do to be saved?" (Acts 16:30). In the A.D. period the question that must eventually take priority is "How can I bring glory to God in all that I eat and drink and in whatever I do?"

Insight From the Courtyard

We see this progression illustrated in even more detail in the three compartments of the Old Testament sanctuary. First, the courtyard ritual answers the B.C. question *What must I do to be saved?* The altar of continual burnt offering, where the animal sacrifice smoldered, represents confession of sin and trust in the Lamb (Jesus) slain to take away the sin of the world (Acts 2:37, 38; 16:31). The bronze laver, where the priest washed in ritual cleansing, represents the baptism by water and spirit of a heart seeking to be cleansed of all sin (John 3:3-6; Titus 3:5).

Insight From the Holy Place

The next question in the progression of Christian experience is *What must I do to* stay *saved?* It's the B.C. question again, but adapted to the A.D. period of life. The concern it represents, namely, maintaining one's own personal salvation, is understandable and normal for the Christian. And the answer is depicted in the holy place of the sanctuary. The table of shewbread, from which the priests ate regularly, represents frequent study of the Word of God for spiritual nourishment and guidance (Matt. 4:4). The golden altar, from which incense continually ascended to God, symbolizes our communication with God (Rev. 8:3). The seven-branched golden candlestick stands for our Christian witness to the world (Matt. 5:14-16).

Insight From the Most Holy Place

And finally we come to the Most Holy Place, where only the high priest could go, and that only once each year on the Day of Atonement. It housed the sacred ark of the covenant containing the Ten Commandments, a pot of manna, and Aaron's rod that had budded. These items represent obedience as a response of love to God's saving initiative (Deut. 10:5, 12, 13), reading Scripture for the primary purpose of communing with Jesus (John 5:39; 6:49-51), and respect for the spiritual leadership He ordains for His people (Num. 17:1-10).

But the chief identifying characteristic of the Most Holy Place was the atonement cover over the ark. From this most sacred place, called the mercy seat, God in all His glorious character would speak to His people (Ex. 25:22; Num. 7:89). Known also as the Shekinah glory, it represented that God was continually among His people and was their ultimate goal. As long as the Shekinah glory remained in the Most Holy Place, it reminded God's people daily that the ultimate purpose of their lives was to bring glory to their God. It identified the ultimate and motivating question for the believer, the priority question of the A.D. period of life: *How can I bring the greatest glory to God through my eating, drinking, and in everything that I do?*

The Priority Question

The problem with the Corinthians was that the wrong question motivated them. They were still obsessed with the question addressed in the holy place, the what-must-I-do-to-stay-saved one. While that's not an invalid question, it can be misapplied to become an end in itself. That's exactly what the Corinthians had done. Therefore, in answer to their question, Can we eat food offered to idols and still be saved? Paul had in essence replied: "You're asking the wrong question. Having set up camp in the holy place, you need to move on to the priority question raised in the Most Holy Place, 'Will eating food offered to idols enable you to bring the greatest glory to God?' And that question has a different answer, one strategically related to our mission as Christians."

Paul's emphasis should be especially significant for us Seventh-day Adventists who believe that in 1844 God riveted our attention on the Most Holy Place of the sanctuary in heaven, and invited us to gain a Most Holy Place experience. A Most Holy Place experience must mean, at the very least, subjecting every area of life to the priority question, "Is God being glorified to the utmost in this area of my life?"

I don't know if Mary's wearing of jewelry will jeopardize her salvation. And I told her so. But I asked her to consider giving up her jewelry for the sake of serving our church in the capacity for which we knew God had gifted her, and for which we needed her. And I am thankful that Mary chose to make that lifestyle adjustment in order to minister through her gifts to our congregation.

In 1 Corinthians 3:13-15 Paul appears to say that God will save some who did not take full advantage of their opportunities to glorify God in their lives. If I knew that I could watch football every Sunday and still be saved, but in the process would miss some special opportunities to bring glory to God, would I still do it? If Jesus has really become the focus of my life, will my primary concern be whether I can watch football and still be saved?

I know what happens to me when Sundays are primarily football from the time the morning paper arrives until the final sportscast on the late news. And I know what it's like to be obsessed all during the week with next Sunday's big game. It's not hard for me to know the answer to the priority question for myself in a situation like that.

But I can't say what's right on these hot-potato-type issues for anyone else but myself. The answers for the items on your list you must wrestle through in the depths of your own heart. That's an essential discipline for today's ordinary Adventist. In part, this is what it means to "work out your salvation with fear and trembling" (Phil. 2:12). But it also means that as you honestly and sincerely subject each item on your list to the priority question, God will be at work "in you to will and to act according to his good purpose" (verse 13).

---

* Leighton Ford, "How to Give an Honest Invitation," *Leadership Magazine,* Spring Quarter 1984, p. 107.

CHAPTER THREE

The Ordinary Adventist's Devotional Life "Desert"

I had been a minister for years and preached regularly about the importance and rewards of Bible study and prayer. Although I had never intentionally tried to deceive anyone about my experience, I do have to admit that based on the selected experiences I had shared in sermons about my devotional life, my parishioners had every reason to believe that my devotional periods were consistently rich and rewarding. Often they were. But the day I confessed that they also often were not, it sent mild shock waves through the Sabbath school class to whom I made the confession. Shock waves, as I later discovered, of relief.

Several members of the class told me privately that they had the same struggle with Bible study and prayer. They felt guilty about it, as though such dry periods called into question the genuineness of their Christian experience. The men and women seemed relieved to hear that their minister, whom they respected, also experienced similar struggles.

Such dry periods, or "desert times," as I refer to them, sometimes last for several days, even weeks. Then comes the temptation "Why keep struggling with something that doesn't work? Do something useful with your time, something that will make a noticeable difference."

Given today's increased time pressures, it is little wonder that we tend to do those things that scream for our attention and will have the most immediate results, pushing into the future any item that doesn't have an immediate, visible payoff.

If one of the items on my daily to-do list is to spend an hour alone with God in some quiet place of my day, who's going to know if I do it or not? What's the immediate payoff? When was the last time anyone asked you Did you spend a thoughtful hour alone with God today?

A major study of Adventist church growth in North America conducted by the Institute of Church Ministry at Andrews University surveyed 8,200 active church members. Forty-one percent reported not having regular personal Bible study and prayer.[1] I'm convinced that most such Adventists who do not seek God in a dedicated time of Bible study and prayer on a daily basis have honestly tried to do so in the past, but ended up scrapping it when it stopped working for them.

Keys to Rewarding Devotions

So what can we do to make our devotional experiences more consistent and rewarding? I've discovered several keys that have helped me immensely.

Key 1: Creative Bible Study

One element of vital devotional experiences is what I call *creative Bible study*. It simply means doing whatever it takes—using sanctified imagination and all possible methods, resources, and means necessary—to make my time spent with God as consistently interesting, rewarding, and productive as possible. Whenever a devotional project I'm working on bogs down or no longer holds my interest, I've learned to move on to another one—another book of the Bible, another devotional book, another method of study, etc. My salvation does not depend upon completing any specific devotional project. If something I've lost interest in is important enough, I can always come back to it later. It's far more important to find something that challenges me presently and keeps drawing me back to the devotional hour so that my time with God will be a daily adventure, rather than something to endure. I take personal responsibility to make my time with God just that.

Another thing I've learned is Don't be in a big hurry! I'm not racing anyone through a devotional project. There's no specific reading assignment that I *have* to get through before Jesus comes. I have the freedom to savor what I read, to allow time for the Holy Spirit to animate it in my imagination, write it in my mind, and seal it in my heart.

Following are some of the things I have done to make my Bible study time productive for me:

1. Reading Scripture by subject has been interesting for me. The first time I remember the Bible becoming really gripping to me was after my conversion, during the summer between my sophomore and junior years at Monterey Bay Academy, when I found myself attracted to portions of Scripture that referred specifically to the second coming of Jesus and the end of the world.

Years later I went through the Bible looking for every scripture I could find on how to know God's will for my life. For the past six months I've been reading what the Bible says about the Holy Spirit. In *How to Be Filled With the Holy Spirit and Know It,* Garrie Williams gives an annotated list of all the Bible texts that mention the Holy Spirit. I've been working my way through that list, making personal notes as I go. It's a wonderful study. The Holy Spirit has become much more personal to me, manifesting as He does the divine quest for intimacy with each of His children.

2. Giving Bible studies to others during my junior year with an academy witnessing team enabled me to learn as I went. During the week I would carefully study the scriptures that we were to teach to the people we were studying with that week. I remember getting up early and going to the only room in the dorm with lights on to study the Bible before the school day began.

3. Modern translations have helped a lot. While attending the seminary, I bought a Revised Standard Version. I couldn't believe the difference it made. It wasn't until then that I read the Bible through for the first time. It took me two years, but the modern translation held my attention.

4. Writing summaries of Bible books often helps me get more out of them. When I went through the entire Bible the first time, I wrote brief summaries of each book on cards that I still have on file and find a useful reference. As I read a Bible book now, I will often jot down a new summary based on new insights I've gained.

5. Cross-referencing as I study has enabled me to understand Scripture better. In several of my Bibles I have written extensive notes to myself in the margins, including related scriptures and insights I've gained on those texts during my study time. Such personalized marginal notes keep the special inspiration of that moment from fading from my memory.

6. Copying all my favorite Bible texts into a journal took me several months. I only got up to Isaiah, but plan to finish the project in the future.

7. Memorizing has been an intriguing challenge at times. I've committed to memory a number of the great hymns in *The Seventh-day Adventist Hymnal.* Recalling one can bring inspiration in the middle of a day. One summer I set a goal of memorizing the book of Hebrews. I got only a few chapters memorized before I lost interest and moved on to another project. Once I took six months to try to memorize the book of Revelation. While I did manage to get most of the chapters memorized, I was never able to repeat more than a few chapters at a time. Yet, to this day, I can visualize in some detail the sequential drama of Revelation from beginning to end.

8. Studying in depth stimulates my interest. While I didn't get Hebrews memorized, I did come back to it later and spent a year studying it verse by verse, writing a personal commentary on it as I went. I didn't consult any printed commentaries on a verse until I had exhausted all the prayerful study I could do on my own, comparing scripture with scripture. Once completed, a study like that never leaves you.

Another time I spent six months exploring the book of John incident by incident, reliving each scene in my imagination. Again, I got the most from it when I wrote out what I was experiencing. I did the same with the book of Matthew, making a detailed outline of every chapter. Then I reviewed the outline repeatedly until I knew where each story and major discourse of Jesus appeared in the gospel.

9. I marked on a map from a Bible atlas all the locations mentioned in David's life as he journeyed from place to place as his story unfolds in 1 and 2 Samuel, 1 Chronicles, and *Patriarchs and Prophets.* Tracking the major events of his life by geography brought his story to life for me.

10. I let one subject lead to another. The study of David's life inspired me to a several-month study of the Psalms. They have been a rich source of spiritual nourishment for me ever since. That study led me to the book of Proverbs. The greatest insights from this book do not lie on the surface for the casual reader, but are like veins of precious ore discovered only by the diligent searcher (Prov. 2:1-6). I spent several challenging months of devotional study trying to systematize Solomon's wisdom sayings by grouping together into one place all the texts that relate to the same subject (how to make friends, how to make wise decisions, how to relate to various kinds of people, how to make wise financial investments, etc.).

11. The writings of Ellen White are excellent devotional material. Besides reading her well-known classics through numerous times, I once spent several months going through the *Testimonies for the Church*. I started with volume nine and worked backward to volume one. That study impressed me with the overall balanced approach to life that emerges when we read widely in her writings. Before I finished the last volume I hit another dry spell and moved on to another project.

12. Interpretative rendering enables me to write out a text, or chapter, or even an entire Bible book in my own words as I think the author might have composed it today. I've attempted this with the entire book of Romans, paraphrasing or interpreting each verse in light of its immediate context as well as its relation to the big picture of the controversy between Christ and Satan. Having worked at this on and off for several years, I am presently up to chapter seven.

13. The focus is on Jesus in every study. But I find it important for me to keep coming back specifically to His life and teachings as recorded in the Gospels and Ellen White's *The Desire of Ages*. Recently I spent many months studying His inaugural address, the Sermon on the Mount, which I consider to be the most concentrated spiritual message ever given to humanity. The six-month study I did on the crucifixion of Jesus changed my thinking and my life forever. During this study, I felt I was standing on holy ground as Moses did at the burning bush. It was as if I was learning to read Scripture again for the first time, and it's never been the same since. That study lifted a veil from my eyes, enabling me to understand and appreciate as never before what God and salvation and religion are all about.

In between some of the more major study projects I've listed above have been many shorter ones—an article someone has given to me, a book of the Bible I've neglected for a while, a devotional book, etc. Sometimes I will turn to something else for a while right in the middle of another project I'm working on, and then return to the larger project within a few days or weeks. Do whatever it takes to keep the devotional hour alive and attractive, and nourishing.

I've learned to accept the message the Bible speaks to me at my present level of understanding and experience, and not to feel guilty because I don't see everything in a text that someone else may. As I pray for the Holy Spirit's guidance, I believe He will lead me to understand what is essential for me now.

I used to feel guilty for losing interest in some projects before I finished them. But I now believe God has used this idiosyncrasy to help me get a balanced spiritual diet over a period of time. A balanced devotional diet is as critical for spiritual health as a balanced nutritional diet is for physical health. For a long time I have felt that a principal reason some people go off the deep end in terms of religious fanaticism is that they fail to achieve a balanced spiritual diet. Wide reading of the Scriptures, as well as in other devotional literature, with a prayerful, humble, receptive spirit, is perhaps the best safeguard possible against deception from extremist views.

Key 2: Creative Prayer

My prayer experience has progressed in tandem with my study experience. When I sense I've gotten into a rut in my prayer life, I try something different. In my daily work organizer (the Day-Timer Executive system), I include a section for my prayer journal. It allows me to add to my prayer list or write out diary-style thoughts to God as needs arise anytime during the day. I can identify with Cardinal John Henry Newman who wrote, "I pray best at the end of a pen."

When I get up in the morning, I begin my time with God by bowing low before Him to prepare my heart to encounter the divine. Confessing my sin, I ask for the anointing of the Holy Spirit for myself and my family, and request divine guidance and intervention in any major situations that I, a family member, or a fellow church member may be facing. Then I may write to God for a while, or add to and review my prayer list, or go directly to Bible study. I have my work organizer close at hand in case I feel prompted to revise my proposed schedule for the day.

On occasion I will review my prayer list for previous months, thanking God for the answers that I and others have received. In the next chapter I will discuss the unanswered prayers, but I have seen too many answers to prayer to discount the integrity of the promises. Answered prayers make the daily Christian walk a dynamic adventure and provide experimental evidence of a living God.

The number of creative ways to pray may be endless. Sometimes I don't ask anything of God, other than a deeper understanding of Him—communing with Him for no other purpose than knowing Him better. Occasionally I enjoy singing hymns of praise to God as part of my prayer experience. I have also sung my own songs of praise to God as they came spontaneously from my heart at the moment. Sometimes I will talk to God as I take a walk. Or I have gone to a park bench somewhere and written a prayer letter to God in that different environment. The different forms of group prayer have especially enriched me. I will sometimes use part of my prayer time to read a new book on prayer. Several books that I have profited from within the last couple of years are Dorothy Eaton Watts's *Prayer Country,* Morris Venden's *The Answer Is Prayer,* Richard Foster's *Prayer: Finding the Heart's True Home,* Roger Morneau's *Incredible Answers to Prayer,* and Joe Engelkemier's *Whatever-It-Takes Praying.*

The true devotional experience does not restrict itself to an hour isolated from the rest of the day. As Thomas Kelly suggests, in the spiritual relationship prayer blends into one with the common acts of life:

"There is a way of ordering our mental life on more than one level at once. On one level we may be thinking, discussing, seeing, calculating, meeting all the demands of our external lives. But deep within, behind the scenes, at a profounder level, we may also be in prayer and adoration, song and worship, and a gentle receptiveness to divine breathings."[2]

Key 3: In Sync With the Rhythm of Life

I visualize the quiet time I spend alone with God as a period when I am aligning myself with the *rhythm of life* as it's manifested in the physical universe and in the lives of Jesus and other notable believers throughout history.

Chicago's renowned Museum of Science and Industry shows a film called *The Power of Ten* that illustrates this rhythm in the physical universe. Using computerized imagery, the camera zooms in 10-power increments from the nucleus of an atom of a human body all the way out to the edge of the observable universe, and then descends again through galaxies and molecular structures to the atom's nucleus. During the film the narrator invites the viewer to note the pronounced rhythmic pattern that characterizes the physical structure of the universe—flurrying activity followed by calm and quiet, repeated over and over in recurring sequences—throughout the journey from the nucleus of the atom to the outer edge of our universe.

Jesus' life exemplified a similar pattern. "Crowds of people came to hear him and to be healed of their sicknesses. But Jesus often withdrew to lonely places and prayed" (Luke 5:15, 16). Such rhythm is essential to spiritual as well as physical life—recurring periods of activity and quiet, accomplishment and solitude, work and prayer. "Prayer and effort, effort and prayer, will be the business of your life."[3] "The life must be like Christ's life—between the mountain and the multitude."[4]

When Luther said, "I have so much to do that I cannot get on without three hours a day of praying," he was aligning himself with the spiritual rhythm of life. I seldom feel it to the depth Luther expressed. But I believe that when I schedule my days so full of activity that I cannot be in tune with the rhythm of life, I violate a fundamental law of my being for which I suffer profound long-term consequences whether or not I immediately perceive them.

Alden Thompson has suggested one of those consequences. He compares prayer to a water filter. Impure water passes through the filter to become clean water. If the filter gets clogged or doesn't filter properly, the water still flows, but it no longer benefits from the purifying effect of the filter.[5] Thompson suggests that the rhythmic periods of solitude, Scripture study, and prayer purify the stream of our lives. Life flows cleaner and purer, in clearer perspective and with deeper meaning, on the other side of those quiet times alone with God. When our time for prayer gets crowded out of our busy schedules, life still goes on. Tasks still get accomplished. But an essential spiritual quality, life's true grace and purpose, is missing.

Key 4: Devotional Ritual

I've discovered that maintaining a set time and place for prayer can make my devotional times with God more profitable. I once heard sociologist Duane McBride cite a study indicating that students who sit in the same seat through an entire quarter, and are allowed to take the final test in that same seat and at the same time period they have been attending the class, generally score higher on the exam than if tested in a different place or time than they're used to. Could it be that we can experience God easier when we have a set ritual, an established time and place to meet Him each day, than when the encounter is erratic and sporadic? I've found that it works that way in my own experience.

Is There a Room in Your Inn?

Ideally, I would give God the best hour of my day. I think of my day as a 24-room hotel, one room for each hour of my day, with my best hour being my executive suite. Each day Jesus comes to me as He did to the little town of Bethlehem 2,000 years ago, seeking a room in my inn, an hour in my day. I'd like Him to have my executive suite.

I'm not a strong morning person. But presently, the hour of my day that has the fewest interruptions and the least distractions is from 6:00 to 7:00 a.m., or thereabouts. That's the time I try to give to God. Sometimes I'm up doing things so late the night before that I'm not alert enough when Jesus comes knocking on my executive suite door. Then I start searching for another room in my day. Some days appointments fill every hour in my day, and I get to the end of the day and realize that Jesus just had no room in my inn that day. I had let a very special opportunity go by. And I used to be so critical of the hotel managers in Bethlehem.

It's not easy to establish a devotional ritual in an age of swing shifts, graveyard shifts, and jam-packed schedules. But regardless of your schedule, you have a best hour in your day, and a next best, and a next, right on down to the hour that's generally numbed with fatigue or filled with so many distractions that you find it hard to concentrate. My advice is: Pick one, slap a reserved sign on it in your appointment book, and allow Him to inhabit it as consistently as you can. You can trust God to help you accomplish the most important things on your list during the remainder of your day (Matt. 6:33).

Stable Time

On those days when some sinister force (sometimes known as staying up to watch *Nightline* or David Letterman the evening before) seems to have wrested your schedule out of your control, remember that Jesus is a very humble God and will take whatever room you offer to Him, even if it's just a stable out back. He isn't one to shame you for being so busy. If your best rooms are filled—if *all* your rooms are filled—then you may hear His still small query, "Might you have a stable out back somewhere?" A few awkward, otherwise unproductive minutes between two appointments, perhaps? Or the few minutes spent at the airport waiting for a plane? Or instead of listening to the radio while driving to the store? Or when the children don't wake up from their nap quite as early as usual? Might there be a stable time somewhere in your day for Him in which He might be born into your day? For our God who inhabits eternity inhabits the stables as well. And as He came forth from the stable of Bethlehem to redeem the world, so He can come forth from the stable times in our days to sanctify our lives.

Dedicated Time Blocks

I have been greatly blessed on the all-too-rare occasions I have reserved a major block of time for God. A few times I have gone on a several-day prayer retreat, seeking a special encounter with God, trying to discern God's perspective on my life and activities, reassessing my priorities for my work, family, and personal life. But some people who can't take time for such extended breakaways have miniperiods of solitude when spouses go on business trips, or when other circumstances provide them with a few extra hours of solace. You could combine such time blocks once or twice a year with a media fast and devote them to seeking a more intimate experience with God. But such occasional blocks of time can never take the place of daily exposure to Bible study and prayer.

Key 5: Prayer About Prayer

A fifth practice that I follow to keep my devotional life vibrant is to pray about it. I ask God to do for me what I can't do to keep our time together rewarding for Him as well as for me. I believe God delights to receive and answer such prayers.

When All Else Fails

I must confess that in spite of all my efforts to keep my devotional experience interesting and rewarding, I still encounter those disheartening "desert" times where the relationship seems to have just gone flat for days, even weeks at a time. At such times I've found two additional practices that help pull me through.

1. Devotional Time Value List

Compiling a list of what the Bible itself says about the importance and value of regular Bible study and prayer, I've identified 17 reasons to not give up on my devotional time with God, regardless of how I'm feeling.

The Bible is: (1) personal communication from God Himself (Heb. 1:1); (2) able to make me wise unto salvation (2 Tim. 3:15); (3) the means through which God has chosen to create spiritual life within me (1 Peter 1:23); (4) the spiritual nourishment that enables me to grow in Christ (Matt. 4:4); (5) the primary means God has chosen to enable me to get to know Jesus, whom to know is to have eternal life (John 5:39 and 17:3); (6) the Spirit's medium for developing the image of Jesus in me (2 Cor. 3:18); (7) the revelation of what God will accomplish in my life when I receive His Word into my life in a humble spirit (Isa. 55:8-11); (8) a guide in helping me make wise decisions (Ps. 119:105); (9) a safeguard that prevents me from slipping into temptation (verse 11); (10) a means of warning and guiding me back to God if I begin to inadvertently stray away from Him (2 Tim. 3:16); (11) a strength to my intellect (Ps. 119:130); and (12) God's training manual, equipping me for effective service (2 Tim. 3:17).

Prayer is: (1) my opportunity to share with God whatever is on my heart (the Psalms); (2) a means of receiving all that God has promised (Matt. 7:7); (3) a channel to bring divine blessing and protection to others whom I care about (Luke 22:31, 32); (4) the release point for all of my anxieties and worries (Phil. 4:6, 7); and (5) two-way communication with God, converting my religion into a relationship (Jer. 33:2, 3).

At times when my devotional life seems to have gone sour, I need only to review the above list to remind myself that time spent seeking God and Jesus through Bible study and prayer holds incredible, wonderful potential.

2. Abandonment

When the desert times come, I've learned not to fight them as hard as I used to. Instead I've tried to learn the spiritual discipline of "abandonment" that those who have lived the most contemplative lives through the centuries have often referred to. Abandonment, as they understood it, simply meant to yield yourself wholly to God and accept with gratefulness whatever He provides. In their contemplative experiences, even the most devout of them encountered the desert experiences, the "dark nights of the soul" as St. John of the Cross referred to them. They learned to accept these dark, seemingly dry, spiritually empty chapters of their lives as gifts from God to be received with gratefulness equal to the periods of spiritual ecstasy.

I had an experience in Las Vegas, during one of its wettest months, that helps me appreciate the accepting spirit of such contemplative Christians. Day after day the rain fell, then the sun would come out and turn the desert as dry as ever. I remarked to a friend that Las Vegas was different than any place I'd ever lived before in that the desert remained barren whether it rained or not. All my friend said in response was "Wait till spring." And sure enough, when spring came the desert blossomed into a gorgeous pageant of wildflowers. My friend found more than 50 varieties in a two-square-foot section of the desert.

That gave me a new perspective on the desert times of my own devotional experience—those times when, try as I may, I just can't seem to get much from my time with God's Word and prayer. Perhaps these desert times are in some sense even a necessary part of growth to full maturity in Jesus Christ. Those periods that seem so dry to me could be the very times that are unusually alive to God beneath the surface. For He assured us that as surely as the rain and snow do not return to their source without bringing forth vegetation, so will His word not return to Him void, but will accomplish the very purpose for which He sent it (Isa. 55:10, 11).

---

[1] Roger L. Dudley and Des Cummings, Jr., "Who Reads Ellen White?" *Ministry,* October 1982, pp. 10-12.

[2] Richard J. Foster, *Celebration of Discipline* (San Francisco: Harper-San Francisco, 1988).

[3] E. G. White, *Our Father Cares,* p. 38.

[4] ———, *Steps to Christ* (Mountain View, Calif.: Pacific Press Pub. Assn., 1956), p. 101.

[5] Alden Thompson, *Inspiration* (Hagerstown, Md.: Review and Herald Pub. Assn., 1991), p. 108.

CHAPTER FOUR

Incredible Unanswered Prayers

In his hymn "Spirit of God" (No. 266 in *The Seventh-day Adventist Hymnal*) George Croly prayed:
> "Teach me to feel that Thou art always nigh;
> Teach me the struggles of the soul to bear;
> To check the rising doubt, the rebel sigh;
> Teach me the patience of unanswered prayer."

"Unanswered prayer"? Have you ever felt the pain and bewilderment of having a very important prayer not get answered in the way you fully expected it to, based on the rules of prayer and the character of God as you understood them? If not, you may do well to skip to the next chapter, because this chapter is for those of us who have.

I sat across the dining room table from Neal, a brilliant teacher of the Christian faith. He had jeopardized his job over a matter of conscience and been fired. Confidently he asked God to help him find another job in his specialized career field. Although he sent his vitae all over the nation, nothing came. Month after month he prayed and searched and waited. Still no response. Now he had called me to his home to tell me he was about to take a job that might compromise his faith and the standards he once held. I will never forget Neal's words to me that day: "If God is my Father as I've always believed and taught, then why didn't He answer me when I needed Him most? I would never treat my children like that. I'm no longer sure there even is a God."

Some people I've shared Neal's story with suspected that he didn't have sufficient faith, or failed to meet some other condition of answered prayer. Like Job's friends, they're sure the problem was with Neal, not with God.

Perhaps the saddest story of unanswered prayer I've come across so far is the one that's recorded in a footnote at the bottom of page 282 of *Selected Messages,* book 2. The son of a missionary family contracted malaria. His parents had read Ellen White's counsel to avoid the use of the drug quinine. So when someone prescribed quinine as the medicine for their son's malaria, his parents chose to put their whole trust in God and prayer for his healing, rather than to compromise and use the drug. Their son subsequently died.

When the couple returned to the States they asked Ellen White what they should have done. She told them they should have administered the drug as well as pray for healing, for "we are expected to do the best we can."

The death of their son could hardly have been the result of a lack of faith on the missionary couple's part. They might be accused of having a misguided faith, but it surely appeared to be sincere faith and perhaps even great faith.

It is not hard to understand why such experiences with prayer can shake a person's religious faith to the very core. And the loss of religious faith that sometimes results ranks among life's most stressful events. David of old testified that unanswered prayers were as traumatic for him as the death of a close friend or relative: "When my prayers returned to me unanswered, I went about mourning as though for my friend or brother. I bowed my head in grief as though weeping for my mother" (Ps. 35:13, 14).

One reason unanswered prayers are so devastating is because of the high expectations raised by such Bible promises as these: "Ask and it will be given to you" (Matt. 7:7). "Whatever you ask for in prayer, believe that you have received it, and it will be yours" (Mark 11:24). Joshua could testify, "Not one of all the good promises the Lord your God gave you has failed. Every promise has been fulfilled; not one has failed" (Josh. 23:14).

While other scriptures qualify these apparent blank checks, we are encouraged as Christians to expect answers to prayer. Christian bookstores carry numerous books filled with stories of answered prayers. One I have, entitled *Prayers God Has Answered,* tells the stories of 30 famous miracle healings through the power of prayer. But I've never seen a book that features stories of unanswered prayers.

The Secret Is Out

Unanswered prayers may be the biggest closet secret of the church. But they are no secret to the Bible. Consider the following representative examples:

The major portion of the book of Job is the story of the patriarch's prolonged period of unanswered prayer for God's intervention to relieve his suffering (see Job 30:20-23).

"All this [calamity] has happened to us," wrote the psalmist, "though we had not forgotten you or been false to your covenant. . . . Why do you hide your face and forget our misery and oppression?" (Ps. 44:17, 24).

Asaph actually accused God of not keeping His promise to Israel: "Will the Lord spurn forever, and never again be favorable? Has his steadfast love ceased forever? Are his promises at an end for all time? . . . And I say, 'It is my grief that the right hand of the Most High has changed'" (Ps. 77:7-10, NRSV).

In Psalm 88 Heman the Ezrahite poured out his bewilderment to God over his unanswered prayers. From childhood he apparently had been afflicted with an ailment that had made him a social outcast. Taught to believe in God and prayer, he petitioned God for healing day after day, year after year, believing that God would hear and answer his prayer. But the deliverance he sought for never came: "O Lord, why do you cast me off? Why do you hide your face from me? Wretched and close to death from my youth up, I suffer your terrors; I am desperate" (verses 14, 15, NRSV).

Paul prayed three times for relief from a serious affliction, but God never removed it (2 Cor. 12:7-9). And in 2 Timothy 4:20 Paul wrote, "I left Trophimus sick in Miletus," and this in spite of the likely possibility that before he left Miletus he would have prayed for healing for his colleague.

Psalm 91 promises, "If you make the Most High your dwelling—even the Lord, who is my refuge—then no harm will befall you, no disaster will come near your tent" (verses 9, 10). But Hebrews 11 speaks of a group of people who made God their refuge, and yet "some were tortured. . . . Others suffered mocking and scourging, and even chains and imprisonment. They were stoned, they were sawn in two, they were killed with the sword; they went about in skins of sheep and goats, destitute, afflicted, ill-treated—of whom the world was not worthy—wandering over deserts and mountains, and in dens and caves of the earth. And all these, though well attested by their faith, did not receive what was promised" (verses 35-40, RSV).

Coping With Unanswered Prayers

What are we to make of these unanswered prayers? And even more important, what are we to make of our own unanswered prayers? After spending years wrestling with these questions, I'm convinced that final answers must await our consultation with God directly in the hereafter. But I have discovered some insights, resources, and practical steps that have helped in this life.

1. Talk Openly to God About Your Disappointment and Disillusionment.

I'm glad it was God Himself who brought this issue of unanswered prayers out of the closet. It was the Holy Spirit who inspired the scriptures we just read that accuse God of not answering prayers and not keeping His promises. What might God possibly have had in mind by allowing such prayers to enter the Bible? I believe it was His way of saying "I understand how much it hurts when you feel I've let you down, and when that happens, I want you to talk to Me about it."

Grief therapists tell us that an important step in recovering from a devastating loss is to acknowledge the hurt we're feeling and to talk to someone about it. Denying the hurt and refusing to discuss it delays, if not prevents, a healthy recovery.

When God's silence has hurt us, it's not only permissible but healthy to tell Him exactly what we're feeling both about the situation and about Him. Repressed feelings of hurt and disillusionment can easily develop into bitterness and a callousness that refuses to pray lest the person get hurt in the same way again. I know of no other way of reconciling with God from the hurt and estrangement caused by unanswered prayer than by talking it through with Him.

That's exactly what Job did. He didn't cover up his pain. He felt God was treating him unfairly, and he told Him so in so many words (Job 6:8, 9). And God said, Job has "spoken of me what is right" (Job 42:7). In other words, God applauded Job for understanding that He was the kind of Person who wanted to hear honestly from Job how he felt, rather than to receive insincere, complimentary, sugar-sweet language from Job that would have masked the grief he felt because he believed that God had betrayed him during his hour of trial.

During times of spiritual discouragement, I have found that if I will share openly with God what I'm honestly feeling, if I will keep talking to Him about it for as long as it takes to get it all out, and if I will then take the time to listen for His still, small, accepting, affirming voice in return, then resolution begins to take place for me even before I gain understanding on the matter, if it ever comes.

2. Seize the Opportunity That Unanswered Prayers Offer to Both Grow in Faith and Honor God.

First Corinthians 10:13 teaches that God will allow no trial to come to us but that at the same time He also will supply us with an equal measure of faith to endure it and conquer it.

Becoming a Christian ensures that there *will be* trials. Through the law of cause and effect, both the righteous and the unrighteous suffer the just consequences of their own mistakes (see Rom. 2:9-11). And the Bible identifies another law, "the law of sin," which unjustly inflicts suffering caused by someone else's mistakes and evil in which the sufferer had no share (Rom. 7:21-25). This is sometimes true in spite of one's prayers for protection. "Beloved, do not be surprised at the fiery ordeal which comes upon you to prove you, as though something strange were happening to you. But rejoice in so far as you share Christ's sufferings, that you may also rejoice and be glad when his glory is revealed" (1 Peter 4:12, 13, RSV).

Could it be that God's promises of protection, such as those in Psalm 91:10, "No evil shall befall you, no scourge come near your tent" (NRSV), apply mainly to protection from spiritual apostasy, rather than from physical harm and danger? Could the primary assurance be that as we continue to earnestly seek God, He will keep our faith from breaking in the hour of trial? The psalmist states, "Many are the afflictions of the righteous, but the Lord rescues them from them all [by strengthening their faith to endure their afflictions successfully?]" (Ps. 34:19, NRSV). While God didn't give Paul the relief he had prayed for from a troubling affliction, He did enable the apostle to grow in faith and honor God through it (2 Cor. 12:7-9). And isn't that what the Christian wants most of all—not merely deliverance from trial, but to remain steadfast in faith and to honor God in the midst of trial?

On the feeling level, Job had no evidence of God's presence. He felt completely forsaken by God, and that all his prayers had gone unanswered. Yet in spite of it all he testified, "Though he slay me, yet will I hope in him" (Job 13:15). "When he has tested me, I will come forth as gold" (Job 23:10). The patriarch's faith had bent but not broken. God had protected him in his hour of trial.

In the end, things worked out for the patriarch. He got back double everything he lost. As far as we know, it wasn't that way for Heman the Ezrahite (Ps. 88). He appears to have gone down to the grave feeling that his prayers had remained unanswered. Yet he still sought the Lord every morning and night, and through the day (verses 1, 13). Perhaps the greatest unsung hero of the Bible, he never gave up.

Through Heman's experience God affirms those who never do gain understanding for their unanswered prayers, and gives them permission to grope in uncertainty even as they seek to be faithful to God as best they know how. As Richard Foster so ably expressed it:

"We may not see the end from the beginning, but we keep on doing what we know to do. We pray, we listen, we worship, we carry out the duty of the present moment. What we learned to do in the light of God's love, we also do in the dark of God's absence. We ask and continue to ask even though there is no answer. We seek and continue to seek even though we do not find. We knock and continue to knock even though the door remains shut. . . .

"It is this constant, longing love that produces a firmness of life orientation in us. We love God more than the gifts God brings. Like Job, we serve God even if he slays us. . . . This is a wonderful grace."[1]

I wonder if Satan understands this yet. Does he grasp the fact that some of us love God for His own sake, even when we don't seem to be getting anything out of it in terms of personal gain or answers to our prayers in ways we had expected? I wonder if he realizes that the power of love is greater than the desire for self-preservation and that even apparent abandonment cannot shake it? He didn't understand it in Job's day, or in Heman the Ezrahite's time. Nor did he grasp it in John the Baptist's day, either.

Early in his ministry John the Baptist drew great crowds. Then Jesus came, and the crowds left John and followed Jesus. John languished in prison without receiving a single visit from Jesus that we know of. If he prayed for deliverance, it never came. And yet his faith did not fail. Shortly before John was beheaded, Jesus testified of him: "Among those born of women there is no one greater than John" (Luke 7:28).

John the Baptist's experience has bequeathed us this profound insight: "Not Enoch, who was translated to heaven, not Elijah, who ascended in a chariot of fire, was greater or more honored than John the Baptist, who perished alone in the dungeon. 'Unto you it is given in the behalf of Christ, not only to believe on Him, but also to suffer for His sake.' Phil. 1:29. And of all the gifts that Heaven can bestow upon men, fellowship with Christ in His sufferings is the most weighty trust and the highest honor."[2]

Highly honored, then, were those unnamed heroes in Hebrews 11:32-40 who went to their death in torture chambers with the words of Psalm 91 quivering on their lips: "If you make the Most High your dwelling . . . no harm will befall you" (verses 9, 10). The Scripture says, "These were all commended for their faith, yet none of them received what had been promised" (Heb. 11:39). Satan thought he could shatter their faith with broken promises. But it didn't work. It never even came close. I can hear God speaking as these men and women, despised and ill-treated by the world, breathed their last: "Well done, My children. I commend you for your great faithfulness. When all the evidence seemed to suggest that I had abandoned you, you stood by Me anyway. Great will be your reward."

3. An Unanswered Prayer Might Be a Blessing in Disguise

Some things we might ask God for in prayer could harm us should God grant them. Only a foolish, irresponsible parent would indulge a child's request to handle matches or to play in the middle of a busy street. Some of our requests could prove equally as dangerous if fulfilled.

Haddon Robinson, president of Denver Seminary, relates a sad conversation he had with a father whose son had just been sentenced to 10 years in a state penitentiary for trafficking in narcotics:

"'You know, I've given him everything he ever asked for,' he said. 'I think that is what destroyed him.'

"That father loved his son. I have no doubt about it. And what the boy asked for he received.

"'I can't hold this back from my son,' I heard him say. 'He knows I have the money to give him whatever he wants.'

"And so the boy was given his heart's desires, but he was destroyed by the gifts."[3]

God is too wise and loves us too much to make such mistakes. "We are so erring and shortsighted that we sometimes ask for things that would not be a blessing to us, and our heavenly Father in love answers our prayers by giving us that which will be for our highest good—that which we ourselves would desire if with vision divinely enlightened we could see all things as they really are."[4]

Romans 8:28 assures us that "in all things God works for the good of those who love him, who have been called according to His purpose." In other words, God will allow nothing to touch my life, including an unanswered prayer, that cannot contribute toward some higher good that I would want to help achieve for God, even at great cost to myself, if I had the choice.

Such assurance, classically immortalized for ordinary Adventists in the following words, has been one of God's greatest gifts to me at those times when I can't make any sense out of what's happening: "God never leads His children otherwise than they would choose to be led, if they could see the end from the beginning, and discern the glory of the purpose which they are fulfilling as coworkers with Him."[5]

4. My Unanswered Prayer Might Benefit Someone Else

During World War II without doubt many sincere German Christians prayed for a speedy end to the war—in favor of the Nazis! Their unanswered prayers benefited the world. Some examples of this kind, however, are not so obvious on the surface.

While I lived in Provo, Utah, I'd always been able to set my garbage out in plastic garbage bags for the weekly garbage pickup. The first time I tried that after moving to a mountainous community near Salt Lake City, neighborhood dogs tore into the bags and strewed garbage all over. When I discovered the price of garbage cans—and wanting to be a good steward—I decided to try a creative alternative involving prayer. So when it came time to set out the garbage again, I told my then 5-year-old son Michael that I was going to show him what God would do to save His tithe-paying children money. We knelt together beside the garbage bags, and I prayed that God would protect them from the dogs, believing that He would do so.

The next morning, as Michael and I were collecting the garbage the dogs had tossed everywhere, I told him that this would be a good lesson for him about how God helps those who help themselves. So the next week on garbage day Michael and I again knelt beside the garbage bags as I prayed that He would protect them from the dogs. Then I sprayed them generously with Raid.

The next morning, while Michael and I again picked up garbage, I told him that Daddy was still learning about prayer. But I thought God had missed a real opportunity.

Perhaps God didn't appreciate me painting Him into a corner as I did. But what's wrong with a father wanting to demonstrate to his son God's reality and the effectiveness of prayer, especially in light of such promises as: "Whatever you ask for in prayer, believe that you have received it, and it will be yours" (Mark 11:24)? As I was grappling with this issue one day, it was as though I heard God saying to me, "Skip, if I had intervened to keep the dogs away from your garbage bags, what would you have done?"

"That's easy, Lord. I would have found a way to work it into my next sermon as a contemporary illustration of Your reality and the power of prayer, just as I was trying to show Michael. I might even have submitted the story to the *Adventist Review*."

"And what do you think those who would have heard and read your story might have been thinking," I could almost hear Him asking in follow-up, "being as most of them probably already owned garbage cans?"

"Well, I don't really know, Lord. I never thought about it that way. I guess they'd think it was a great story. But then, too, I suppose some of them might have felt as if they didn't have much faith compared to me. Come to think of it, if I had seen one of them in K Mart the next week buying a new garbage can, I might have been tempted to think, *Oh, ye of little faith.* Ah-ha! I think I'm beginning to understand."

With all due respect to my sincerity and faith (which was at least mustard-seed size), I now understand that had God intervened to protect my garbage bags it might have had a detrimental effect for others that far outweighed the benefits I was seeking.

What if God had intervened to heal the little missionary boy whose parents chose not to give him the prescribed medicinal drug, quinine? Might other believers thereby have been encouraged to ignore professionally prescribed medicines and treatments in cases of serious illness? Some might even have concluded that they would be sinning to even consult a doctor.

In the scriptural promise of divine healing associated with the anointing service (James 5:14, 15), the word used for the anointing oil was the same word used for the medicinal oil of that day (cf. Luke 10:34). This may imply that when praying for healing, we should also cooperate to the best of our ability with God's own commitment to His natural, orderly laws of cause and effect.

5. Consult the Evidence From the Past
When Jesus hung on the cross, He felt completely abandoned— "My God, my God, why hast thou forsaken me?" (Matt. 27:46, KJV). Even though on the intellectual level He was aware of the Old Testament promises that He would be resurrected, on the feeling or emotional level it seemed to Him that He would be lost forever. He "could not see through the portals of the tomb. Hope did not present to Him His coming forth from the grave a conqueror, or tell Him of the Father's acceptance of the sacrifice."[6]

Jesus' own experience of feeling eternally lost, even when He wasn't, helps me understand why it often doesn't help someone who's experiencing the devastation of unanswered prayer to tell them that there's no such thing as unanswered prayer. For in a time of severe crisis, what may be true conceptually may not be capable of being perceived emotionally.

When Jesus felt totally abandoned by God and lost forever, He sustained His faith by recollecting God's acceptance of Him in the past. "In those dreadful hours He had relied upon the evidence of His Father's acceptance heretofore given Him."[7]

After Asaph accused God of not keeping His promise (Ps. 77:7-10), he said, "I will call to mind the deeds of the Lord; I will remember your wonders of old" (verse 11, NRSV). Then, as Jesus did, he recounted specific evidences of God's blessings to him and his people in the past (verses 16-20).

All of us have had experiences and blessings that we accepted at the time as unmistakable indications of God's love and care for us. And at such times when it seems as though God is not responding, we, like Asaph and Jesus, can draw strength from recalling those evidences of our Father's acceptance that He has already given us.

God's Ironic Response

I believe that if we rightly understood all God's promises as God meant them, we could affirm: "His promises will be fulfilled. They have never failed; they can never fail."[8] At the same time, that doesn't deny the legitimate feelings of disappointment, pain, and anger that we sometimes need to work through with God when all the evidence of our senses suggests that He has abandoned us.

As ironic as it may seem, when we accuse God of breaking His promises, He responds with more promises, heaping promise upon promise. On the surface it doesn't make any sense. But for some of us, it works.

"The Lord has forsaken me, my Lord has forgotten me" (Isa. 49:14, RSV). That's the way it feels when we conclude an important prayer has gone unanswered. And when God heard His people talking like that, expressing their loss of faith in Him and His promises, He didn't scold them for what they were feeling and saying. He just came right back at them with another consoling promise: " 'Can a woman forget her sucking child, that she should have no compassion on the son of her womb?' Even these may forget, yet I will not forget you" (verse 15, RSV).

"I will never leave you or forsake you" (Heb. 13:5, NKJV). "I will be with you always" (Matt. 28:20, TEV). How do you stay angry with a God who keeps coming on like that?

Sometimes He asks us only to hold on until the Great Day when it will all make sense:

"All that has perplexed us in the providences of God will in the world to come be made plain. The things hard to be understood will then find explanation. The mysteries of grace will unfold before us. Where our finite minds discovered only confusion and broken promises, we shall see the most perfect and beautiful harmony. We shall know that infinite love ordered the experiences that seemed most trying."[9]

In the world to come, "we shall see that our seemingly unanswered prayers and disappointed hopes have been among our greatest blessings."[10]

[1] Richard J. Foster, *Prayer: Finding the Heart's True Home* (San Francisco: Harper-San Francisco, 1992), pp. 24, 25.

[2] E. G. White, *The Desire of Ages*, p. 225.

[3] Haddon Robinson, *The Solid Rock Construction Company* (Grand Rapids: Discovery House Publishers, 1989), p. 106.

[4] E. G. White, *Steps to Christ*, p. 96.

[5] ———, *The Desire of Ages*, p. 224.

[6] *Ibid.*, p. 753.

[7] *Ibid.*, p. 756.

[8] ———, *Steps to Christ*, pp. 111, 112.

[9] ———, *Our Father Cares*, p. 67.

[10] ———, *The Ministry of Healing* (Mountain View, Calif.: Pacific Press Pub. Assn., 1905), p. 474.

LOOKING AT ONE ANOTHER

GOSSIP divorce

lifestyle

hurts

CHAPTER FIVE

Sometimes It Hurts More to Be in Church

The church is a place where people get hurt. For this reason I have often thought of the church as the worst idea God ever had, the biggest mistake He ever made.

Have you ever been hurt by the church? If you haven't, I suspect you haven't been in it long enough yet, because it seems to come with the territory of being an ordinary Adventist. Members are misunderstood, falsely accused, taken advantage of, unjustly criticized, overworked, underappreciated, etc. And when it happens, the hurt can go very deep. We don't mean to injure each other, but we do. For this reason I believe that responsible preparation of baptismal candidates today should include instruction on how to relate to such wounds when they occur. To provide deeper understanding of such hurts and how to grow through them is the purpose of this chapter and the next.

During the Desert Storm military mission in Iraq, news reports came of U.S. military casualties accidentally caused by other U.S. soldiers. They called it "friendly fire"—being wounded or killed by one's friends. "Friendly fire" can inflict the deepest of all injuries. Experiencing it himself, David expressed anguish of heart: "If an enemy were insulting me, I could endure it; if a foe were raising himself against me, I could hide from him. But it is you, a man like myself, my companion, my close friend, with whom I once enjoyed sweet fellowship as we walked with the throng at the house of God" (Ps. 55:12-14).

I believe that many inactive Adventists are casualties of "friendly fire." When wounded by the church, they didn't stop believing the Adventist message, but it came to the place where it hurt too much to stay in it. I've known such injuries to go so deep that the response was extreme.

I knew Shaun when he was a junior in academy. The previous summer he had gone on a student mission project overseas. Someone asked him to give a vesper report on his mission experience. It wasn't the most polished presentation I'd ever heard, but it was sincere. The students seemed unusually restless that evening, and several made quite vocal and demeaning comments during his report. A couple weeks later a stunned student body watched paramedics transport Shaun's lifeless body from the dorm to the ambulance. The autopsy report concluded that his death was self-inflicted.

Shaun had not confided in anyone to give us a clue as to what ultimately led to his desperate act. His was a silent death, like the fish in my aquarium that show no symptoms of illness until I find them floating lifeless on top of the water. I don't know if that vesper program contributed to it. But we never know how much someone in the church may be hurt by our seemingly innocent critical remarks and carelessness.

God alerted me to this in a dream that involved Don, a student I was having classes with in college. Don slept through every class we had together. When the teacher asked him a question, I woke him and told him the wrong question, to which he waxed eloquent to the sadistic enjoyment of myself and others in the class. When Don discovered my practical joke, he laughed with us. In my dream my class members and I were little children playing cowboys. I aimed a plastic squirt gun at Don and pulled the trigger. Instead of water, real bullets came out and hit him. He fell, bleeding, but laughing as if he were still enjoying the game. When I woke up I inquired around about Don and discovered that he was making a career change so he could be a missionary, and had to work 40 hours a week at nights to pay tuition. I repented and tried to be a support to him from that day on.

Eventually Don got to the mission field, surviving the hurts we inflicted. Shaun didn't. And while Shaun's reaction was extreme and rare, anytime an ordinary Adventist withdraws from active involvement or becomes an inactive-member casualty due to "friendly fire," it's an equal tragedy. And in most cases it's avoidable.

Tracking the Transition

John Savage's research identified the stages in the progression from active to inactive member status.

1. Hurt Inflicted

First, some injury occurs—being criticized or wronged by a fellow member, having a confidence betrayed, unresponsiveness of fellow members to one's deep-felt spiritual needs, a conflict with the pastor, feeling one's willingness to serve taken advantage of, discomfort with changes taking place in the church, discovery of disturbing problems in the church, or any number of other possibilities. The perceived source of hurt may even be imaginary, but the hurt itself remains real and very painful.

Church wounds are often complex and unintended. I well remember my involvement with one of the visitation teams calling on nearly 200 former or inactive members in our area. We discovered that the majority had stopped coming to church during a time of severe personal or family crisis that often involved a marital estrangement or separation. Often both members of an estranged couple would continue attending church for a time. But eventually the pain of the estrangement, the discomfort of sitting in church alone when they used to enjoy the "normality" of being coupled, the awkwardness of trying to relate to church members who didn't know what was appropriate to say to them anymore, and the sense of being rejected by other members (whether the rejection was real or imagined only God knows), became more than they could deal with on top of everything else.

2. Cry for Help

Somewhere along the line the wounded member gives a cry for help, quite often expressed in such comments as "Our church seems so cold and indifferent these days"; "Our members don't seem to care as much as they used to"; "I just can't do this job anymore"; "The pastor's sermons are so dry"; "I'm burned out and don't think I'll accept any church responsibilities next year"; etc. When such cries occur, it's vital that the church respond. Often a listening ear and compassionate understanding, assuring them that others do care, is what the person needs. We may compare wounded members in this stage to sheep that wander from the flock and can't find their own way back. They will bleat their distress cries, then listen for answering bleats from the flock. If responses aren't forthcoming, the lost sheep keep wandering farther away from the fold.

3. Change of Behavior

If their cries for help continue to go unnoticed or remain ignored, changes in patterns of church attendance, faithfulness in meeting church obligations, financial giving, etc., often occur. Such changes of behavior are actually intensified cries for help. If no one from the congregation notices and responds to them, the final stage often results.

4. Readjustment to Life Outside the Church

In this final stage former members reinvest their time, talents, and finances in their families and causes outside the church. Savage maintains that in order for the church to reclaim members during the final two stages, it must be willing to listen patiently, acceptingly to the stories of their hurts, ask forgiveness for the church's contribution to their injuries, and assure them that they are genuinely wanted and would be accepted back again.

An Idea God Couldn't Stop

The church may have been a bad idea when viewed exclusively from its potential for people to get hurt. But one thing's for sure—God would have had to make a commandment against the church to keep it from happening. Because people like to get together with other people who believe as they do, do the things they like to do, and want to accomplish the same things they want to accomplish. Thus the different clubs it's possible to belong to—astronomy clubs, sports fan clubs, African violet clubs, model train clubs, Lions and Kiwanas clubs, Democratic and Republican parties, and thousands of other social groups. Even if God had made a commandment against people getting together in His name for prayer, study, and worship, someone likely would have broken the commandment and started the church anyway.

But God didn't give a commandment against the church—He did just the opposite. Jesus said He was the one who built the church and chose it to be His visible body on earth through which He would work to bless the world as He did through His human body when He lived here (Matt. 16:18; Eph. 1:22, 23). In obedience to Christ, wherever the gospel spread, local and regional congregations sprang up for study, prayer, worship, and witness (Rom. 16:1; 1 Cor. 1:2; 16:19; etc.).

Outweighing the Hurts

Jesus knew full well that the church would be a community in which people would get hurt, and yet He formed it Himself and called all believers to be actively involved in it. Obviously, He must have found the benefits of belonging to the church sufficient to outweigh the drawbacks.

If you've been seriously wounded in your relationship with the church, I appeal to you not to give up on the church for the following reasons:

1. The Inspiration of Godly Lives

When Jesus went to church, He sat down the pew from people who tried to throw Him out, hypocrites He knew would ultimately seek to kill Him. His church hurt Him badly. And yet Luke 4:16 tells us that He went to church every Sabbath of His life. What kept Him going?

There seemed to be something about worshiping His Father with other believers that drew Him like a magnet: "I will declare your name to my brothers; in the presence of the congregation I will sing your praises" (Heb. 2:12). While hypocrites and people who hurt Him severely attended His church, there was also a widow there, giving her last coins in thanksgiving for God's goodness to her; there was a publican there who, unlike the proud hypocrites, wouldn't even look up as he sought God's forgiveness and cleansing; there was a recovering harlot there who believed in Him and was saving up a whole year's wage to buy Him a fragrant gift in gratitude for her deliverance; the hospitality chairwoman was there, the one with the heart of gold who loved to feed Him, but who still worried over many things with a fretful heart that He longed to quiet; His 12 companions were there, jealously infighting for first place in His attention, but who still believed in Him and in the transformation He was making in their lives. Jesus drew strength and inspiration from them and like worshipers.

Every congregation has such people—struggling sinners, to

be sure—but whose very presence there is a miracle in itself. Their persistent quest to be like Jesus is a source of inspiration and encouragement.

The Oxford scholar and professor C. S. Lewis wrote: "When I first became a Christian, about 14 years ago, I thought that I could do it on my own, by retiring to my room and reading theology, and I wouldn't go to the churches. . . . I disliked very much their hymns, which I considered to be fifth-rate poems set to sixth-rate music. But as I went on I saw the great merit of it. I came up against different people of quite different outlooks and different education, and then gradually my conceit just began peeling off. I realized that the hymns (which were just sixth-rate music) were, nevertheless, being sung with both devotion and benefit by an old saint in elastic-side boots in the opposite pew, and then you realize that you aren't fit to clean those boots. It gets you out of your solitary conceit."[1]

2. Healing Occurs

While the church is the place where people get hurt, it's also where the wounds get healed. I have watched the church rally around people in crisis, and it's done the same for me. If the church was one of God's worst ideas for the hurt that it sometimes causes, it was also one of His best ideas for the healing that it brings.

When a herd of American buffalo were threatened, they formed a circle with the bulls standing shoulder to shoulder, facing outward toward the enemy, and the calves and females huddled within. The only ones in danger were those who broke from the group and charged out to face the enemy alone. I believe there is a parallel here to the importance of staying by the church when the hurts come.

Jesus specified a series of progressive steps that His followers should take to achieve healing where threatening conflict occurs between members in the church, or to restore those whose careless-ness has placed their spiritual welfare in jeopardy (Matt. 18:15-17). These steps, which are both reconciling and disciplinary in nature, are so important for establishing a healing climate within the church that, rather than try to discuss them in a few paragraphs here, I am devoting my next chapter in its entirety to them. Sometimes the church's efforts to fulfill this divine mandate inad-vertently and unavoidably causes even more hurt for the very members they're trying to help. "No discipline seems pleasant at the time, but painful. Later on, however, it produces a harvest of righteousness and peace for those who have been trained by it" (Heb. 12:11). Like a surgeon, the church must sometimes wound in order to bring deeper healing. And members so wounded should be treated with the same attention, support, love, and care that we give to postsurgical patients in intensive-care units.

3. A Safe Place to Get Hurt

Perhaps God decided that since relational injuries will occur inevitably in a world of sin, what people needed most was a caring environment where hurts could occur safely and where people could learn to work them through to resolution. If so, then we may view the wounds that sometimes come through one's involvement with the church as creating a new level of potential for personal growth.

4. Recovery in Process

Jesus Christ resides in the church ("where two or three come together in my name, there am I with them" [Matt. 18:20]) to restore recovering sinners into His own image and likeness ("to make her holy, cleansing her by the washing with water through the word, and to present her to himself as a radiant church, without stain or wrinkle or any other blemish, but holy and blameless" [Eph. 5:26, 27]).

People get hurt in the church because God chose to form it out of recovering sinners, ordinary Adventists like me, who will be swimming upstream against our sinful natures until Jesus returns. Each time I relapse into my old selfish ways, allowing my sinful nature to carry me back downstream, other people get injured in the process. The church is the place where Jesus works to transform His children into people who won't keep hurting others.

Floyd Bresee tells of a time he had to rush his wife to the emergency room. A poster on the wall of the entrance to the hospital read "The Hurt Stops Here." He says that sign should hang over the entrance to all of our churches.

I wish that were possible. So does Jesus. I want to be part of such a church when it happens. So I choose to stay in the church—even though I know I will get hurt—to undergo the spiritual discipline of close interaction with other recovering sinners who are very different from me in many ways, to learn to work through the disagreements and differences, and to discover together how to share His love with others until that day He finishes molding His church to stand before Him without wrinkle or blemish, bearing His own image and character.

I like the pragmatic way this sentiment is recognized and expressed in the following poem I once heard Linda Shelton read that's a loose takeoff from Joyce Kilmer's well-known "I Think That I Shall Never See a Poem as Lovely as a Tree":

I think that I shall never see a church that's all it ought
    to be,
A church whose members never stray beyond the strait
    and narrow way;
A church that has not empty pews, whose pastor never
    has the blues;
A church whose deacons always seek, and none is proud
    and all are meek;
Where gossips never peddle lies, or make complaints or
    criticize;
Where all are always sweet and kind, and all to others'
    faults are blind.
Such perfect churches there may be, but none of them
    are known to me.
So I'll just work and pray and plan to make my own the
    best I can.

5. Word of God Honored

The church reveres and studies the Word of God. Sabbath school classes follow a curriculum to expose members to the Word of God in its entirety. Scripture is the focus of attention in the weekly worship service as sermons attempt to apply it to our daily lives. The Word of God is often the reference point in personal conversations and fellowship between church members. Within the church we attempt to center our lives on the Word. To be sure, we often fail at it, but forces built into the very nature of the church itself keep drawing us back again and again to the converting, transforming, healing Word of God.

6. Prayer Is Made

People in the church pray together and for each other. When Paul arrived at Philippi, he asked if anyone knew where people met on the Sabbath to pray (Acts 16:13). He wanted to be there. When people gather for prayer, something happens. Jesus said, "If two of you on earth agree about anything you ask for, it will be done for you by my Father in heaven" (Matt. 18:19). When you're a member of the church, the only way to keep off someone's prayer list as you go through a crisis is not to let others know what you're experiencing. Because many people in the church believe in prayer and are great pray-ers. The prayers of the church have meant much to me at difficult times of my life.

7. Presence Makes a Difference

No Bible text tells us to go to church to receive a blessing. If the primary reason I go to church is to obtain a blessing, I'm likely to fall away when I'm hurt in it. Instead, we're instructed to go to church to "encourage one another" (Heb. 10:25) and to "spur one another on toward love and good deeds" (verse 24).

How do you encourage others when you go to church? I'd like to suggest that your very presence helps others. Beyond that, if you notice someone who looks as though they're going through a difficult time, you could speak a word of encouragement, or call on them during the week to assure them of your prayers. If you've ever been hurt by the church and worked it through to resolution, then you are in a position to assist others when they get hurt (2 Cor. 1:3, 4).

8. Witness for God Takes Place

Jesus ordained the church to carry on the work for others that He began (Matt. 28:19, 20). The Holy Spirit has endowed you with one or more spiritual gifts that, when used in cooperation with others in the church, can result in a greater ministry and witness for God than if you were merely serving Him alone (Rom. 12:3-8; 1 Cor. 12; Eph. 4:1-16; etc.). One of the great adventures in the Christian life is found in working together to make the greatest present and eternal difference in the lives of others that we possibly can.

The Forgiveness Connection

If the church has hurt you, you cannot heal or grow until you can forgive. Marjorie Thompson's definition of forgiveness has been most helpful for me:

"To forgive is to make a conscious choice to release the person who has wounded us from the sentence of our judgment, however justified that judgment may be. It represents a choice to leave behind our resentment and desire for retribution, however fair such punishment might seem. It is in this sense that one may speak of 'forgetting'; not that the actual wound is ever completely forgotten, but that its power to hold us trapped in continual replay of the event, with all the resentment each remembrance makes fresh, is broken."[2]

Stages of Forgiveness

In his book *Forgive and Forget* Lewis Smedes identifies four stages in the forgiveness process. First, we hurt. If we deny the hurt, it's hard to get past it. Second, we hate. Some of us have a hard time accurately labeling such emotions toward an offender when we've been hurt. But the hating stage is a normal one in the recovery process for most of us. Third, we heal. Smedes suggests that you can know you have really forgiven someone when you can hear their name and instinctively and honestly wish them well. And finally you come together with the offender to make peace as far as possible. It may not be possible to renew the relationship at the level that once existed, but an attempt to achieve reconciliation at some level is important. Once the attempt at reconciliation and discussion of the appropriate form of a modified relationship with the other party has been sincerely made, personal closure is possible regardless of how the other party responds.

The Five Steps of Forgiveness

I have discovered five steps that lead to forgiveness:

1. **Accept your need to forgive.** Jesus not only commanded us to forgive, but even said that unless we forgive those who offend us, we will not be forgiven ourselves (Matt. 6:12-15; 18:21-35). When you've been deeply hurt, it's an illusion to think that you can just ignore it or live around it, for the memory of that injury will keep you tethered to its pole until forgiveness occurs. If you fail to do the work necessary to achieve forgiveness, you enslave yourself to your offender.

2. **Acknowledge your inability to forgive.** When Jesus' accusers questioned His right to forgive sins, Jesus asked them which was easier, to forgive someone or to heal them? (See Mark 2:5-12.) For many of us, it's as impossible to forgive those who have sinned

against us as it would be for us to heal them. That's not true of every offense. But you will know when you've come up against something that's bigger than you are—when the hurt keeps replaying in your memory, with its accompanying emotions, and you seem powerless to prevent it. Then the only way to get past that point is to acknowledge that we cannot forgive. Such confession can drive us to the third step.

3. **Ask God to give you a forgiving spirit.** Jesus said, "Ask, and it will be given to you" (Matt. 7:7). God is by nature a forgiver—even as men nailed Jesus to the cross, He prayed for their forgiveness (Luke 23:34). And He will grant us that same forgiving spirit toward those who hurt us when we ask Him for it (Eph. 4:32; Acts 5:31).

4. **Yield all bitterness and desire for revenge to God.** Dr. Hans Selye, the world's leading authority on stress management, identified the desire for revenge as the most damaging of all human emotions. The Lord says, "It is mine to avenge; I will repay" (Rom. 12:19). As we release the desire for revenge to God, we begin to experience freedom from the self-enslavement of bitterness. Lewis Smedes said, "To forgive is to set a prisoner free, and then discover that the prisoner was you."[3]

5. **Do good toward your offenders.** "Do not repay anyone evil for evil, . . . But overcome evil with good" (Rom. 12:17-21). "Love your enemies and pray for those who persecute you, so that you may be children of your Father in heaven; for he makes his sun rise on the evil and on the good, and sends rain on the righteous and on the unrighteous" (Matt. 5:44, 45, NRSV). When you can genuinely act with benevolence toward those who have hurt you deeply, you will experience the exhilaration of Jesus' words, "If the Son sets you free, you will be free indeed" (John 8:36).

The Cadillac and the Church

Morris Vendon relates a parable about a Cadillac dealer in southern California who had the greatest grand opening on record. The first 10 people who came on opening day were each to get a new Cadillac. Vendon got in line two days early. In spite of the pushing and jockeying that occurred as the moment for the opening neared, he maintained his place at the front of the line, until he saw his friend David close behind him. David had often criticized

Vendon, especially for Vendon's interest in Cadillacs. Now, here David was trying to get a free one for himself. Vendon thought, *If critics and hypocrites like David are going to be driving around in one of these free Cadillacs, you can count me out!* Whereupon he went home.

Should I leave the church because hypocrites and people who have hurt me are in it, I would be removing myself from the very environment Jesus dwells in to transform recovering sinners like myself into His own image and likeness to prepare them for eternity. People who stay by their church to work through their hurts, to learn from and contribute all they can through their church, turn out to be some of the most beautiful people on earth. Jesus said such people are His joy and delight (Ps. 16:3). Like rose petals that have been crushed, their lives bear the irresistible fragrance of His character and love in the world.

---

[1] C. S. Lewis, *God in the Dock* (Grand Rapids, Mich.: William B. Eerdmans Publishing Company, 1970), pp. 61, 62.

[2] Marjorie Thompson, "Moving Toward Forgiveness," *Weavings,* March/April 1992, p. 19.

[3] Lewis Smedes, "Forgiveness: The Power to Change the Past," *Christianity Today,* January 7, 1983, p. 26.

CHAPTER SIX

The Great Adventist Climate-Buster

Having gotten the issue of being hurt by the church out into the open, I must now share with you what I consider to be the scourge of the church.

Ideally, as we have noted previously, the church should provide a safe climate for people—a place they're not going to get hurt, a place they will be accepted and respected and allowed to grow at their own pace, a place they can receive loving guidance and protective warning away from behavior harmful both to themselves and others.

As we have also noted, the reason the church doesn't have a safer climate than it does is that God formed it out of recovering sinners, like yours truly, who are capable of instant relapses. He's also instructed us to get together regularly for worship and witness, and there's the rub, because anytime recovering sinners gather for any length of time, someone inevitably gets hurt.

The potential the church has for injuring members didn't catch Jesus by surprise. In fact, He gave a commandment that anticipated our sinful relapses and most of the other occasions for wounding within the church. If we strictly followed this commandment, it would convert occasions of hurt into opportunities for personal growth, maturing, and healing. I believe that God expected His last-day church, "who obey God's commandments and remain faithful to Jesus," would be a model community based on this commandment (Rev. 14:12). But the scourge of the church, the great Adventist safe-climate buster, is the extent to which this very commandment—the one that could transform the church as problem into the church as promise—may have become the most neglected commandment of all.

The Context

Before we put a magnifying glass to this commandment, recorded in Matthew 18:15-17, let's note its wider context:

Matthew 18:1-5: Jesus expresses His deep love for children. "Unless you change and become like little children," He said, "you will never enter the kingdom of heaven." He asks us to be like children—teachable, trainable, willing to learn, grow, develop, and mature.

Matthew 18:6-10: Jesus said to be very careful how you relate to the children—not merely those young in years, but spiritual children who are young in faith. "If anyone causes one of these little ones who believe in me to sin, it would be better for him to have a large millstone hung around his neck and to be drowned in the depths of the sea." It's apparent that Jesus feels very strongly about this! He hates needless offenses.

Matthew 18:11-14: People offended and hurt in their relation to the church sometimes end up leaving the church, and even worse, sometimes turn their backs on Jesus Himself. Jesus leaves no doubt that His chief mission is to find those wandering members and bring them back.

Matthew 18:15-17: Here we find Jesus' climate-building commandment that we will examine in detail momentarily, and which if followed strictly, would make the church the safest, most nurturing place on earth.

Matthew 18:17, 18: When an erring member of the church refuses all attempts for reconciliation and restoration, apparently having turned his or her back on God and the church, Jesus invites and empowers the church to officially acknowledge that reality through the act of disfellowshipping, so that the person might know where he or she stands in relation to the church.

Matthew 18:19, 20: Jesus promises to be especially with those who pray together for the resolution of conflict within the church and for the restoration of alienated members. I believe this promise applies especially to those who pray that God will write this commandment on their hearts that they might not become a source of offense for others.

Matthew 18:21-35: The parable of judgment on the servant forgiven an enormous debt, but who refused to forgive his debtor, reveals that the healing that comes from having our own sins forgiven depends, to a significant degree, on the extent to which we offer that same forgiveness to those who hurt us.

The Climate Builder

Now to the climate-building commandment itself: "If another member of the church sins against you, go and point out the fault when the two of you are alone. If the member listens to you, you have regained that one. But if you are not listened to, take one or two others along with you, so that every word may be confirmed by the evidence of two or three witnesses. If the member refuses to listen to them, tell it to the church; and if the offender refuses to listen even to the church, let such a one be to you as a Gentile and a tax collector" (Matt. 18:15-17, NRSV).

I've discovered the hard way that whenever I violate the sacred order Jesus outlined here, it will always lead to harmful consequences. I'm going to walk us through this commandment phrase by phrase.

"If another member of the church sins against you . . ." (verse 15). It's really not a matter of "if," but more likely a matter of "when." But Jesus still hopes and works for the ideal—a congregation that's developed a climate that's completely safe and isn't needlessly wounding people anymore. He longs for members who reach a spiritual maturity where "offenses" committed against them don't derail them as they once did. So for Jesus, the eternal optimist, it's still "if" rather than "when."

Some ancient manuscripts do not have the words "against you" in this text. In that case the text would read "If another member of the church sins . . ." This would apply if you were to see me doing something that you believe threatens my spiritual welfare or that of others. It calls for members to take an interest in each other's spiritual welfare. At first glance this may appear to give free license to someone with a fanatical bent to prey on other members, but as the commandment unfolds it contains sufficient checks and balances to make it safe for application. Jesus strictly enjoined us not to judge each other (Matt. 7:1-5). But He does not want a climate in the church that welcomes new members, but then shows no interest in their continuing spiritual welfare.

The commandment unfolds in three progressive levels.

Level One: Between the Two of You

"Go and point out the fault when the two of you are alone" (Matt. 18:15, NRSV). This defines the first level of response to personal offense or to behavior that jeopardizes someone's spiritual development. Solomon had given the same instruction earlier: "Argue your case with your neighbor directly, and do not disclose another's secret" (Prov. 25:9, NRSV).

We can already see that it is not an easy commandment. God has asked us to do a hard thing. I can think of many less difficult ways to try to resolve conflict situations than in the way Jesus commanded. If you hurt me, or if I see you doing something I believe is spiritually detrimental to yourself or others, it would be much easier for me to tell someone else about it, and hope that they might speak to you about it—someone not so involved, perhaps, or who knows you better than I do, or who would seem to be better qualified to discuss such things with you. I could divulge the matter to the members of my small prayer group and ask them to pray about it. But the climate-building commandment rules out such responses.

Jesus is very protective of your reputation. He wants me to go to you alone, and resolve it between the two of us, so that no one else ever has to know about it. In the outside world, if you make a serious mistake and some reporter can scoop the story, it's the banner headline of tomorrow morning's newspaper. But Jesus ordained the church to be a place it's safe for you to make a mistake, a place we care enough about each other that we will go to each other humbly, prayerfully, to discuss it just between the two of us, a place mistakes are allowed to be privately repented of rather than publicly exposed.

Knowing When to Go

How do you know when something is significant enough to talk to another member about? Jesus said: "When you are offering your gift at the altar, if you remember that your brother or sister has something against you, leave your gift there before the altar and go; first be reconciled to your brother or sister, and then come and offer your gift" (Matt. 5:23, 24, NRSV). I also use another criterion: If something transpires between you and me that has adversely affected my ability to regard you as a Christian brother or sister, then I need to do something about it. If I'm not willing to talk to you directly, then neither should I talk to anyone else about the matter.

Perhaps what I need is to pray for my own ability to overcome the negative attitude I carry toward you. Or I may need to pray for the Christian maturity to go to you personally and discuss the matter between the two of us alone.

If I'm allowed to talk to someone else about something I hold against you, then it's easy for me to consider the matter serious enough to talk about. But if I commit myself to do nothing in any line that would violate Jesus' climate-building commandment to speak only to the individual involved, then in many cases I've found that the matter really seemed quite petty after all. I've been able to resolve many such issues within the confines of my own heart.

How to Respond to Gossip

What should you do if someone comes to you with an evil report about another person? Consider this straight counsel:

"Ministers and lay members of the church displease God when they allow individuals to tell them the errors and faults of their brethren. They should not listen to these reports, but should inquire: 'Have you strictly followed the injunctions of your Saviour? Have you gone to the offender and told him of his faults between you and him alone? And has he refused to hear you? Have you carefully and prayerfully taken two or three others, and labored with him in tenderness, humility, and meekness, your heart throbbing with love for his soul?' If the Captain's orders, in the rules given for the erring, have been strictly followed, then an advance step is to be taken—tell it to the church, and let action be taken in the case according to the Scriptures. . . . If these steps have not been taken, close the ear to complaints, and thus refuse to take up a reproach against your neighbor."[1]

"Speak evil of no man. Hear evil of no man. If there be no hearers, there will be no speakers of evil. If anyone speaks evil in your presence, check him. Refuse to hear him, though his manner be ever so soft and his accents mild. He may profess attachment, and yet throw out covert hints and stab the character in the dark.

"Resolutely refuse to hear, though the whisperer complains of being burdened till he speak. Burdened indeed! With a cursed secret which separateth very friends. Go, burdened ones, and free yourselves from your burden in God's appointed way. [Matthew 18:15-17 is quoted at this point.]"[2]

I believe we should heed Mrs. White's counsels even in our prayer groups. Damaging gossip can be pretentiously cloaked in the garment of prayer. Should not our prayer groups be the safest of all environments in terms of protecting each other's reputations in God's appointed way?

The Climate Buster

What damage occurs when I pass on or listen to an evil report about you? First, if someone gives me a negative report about you, it's unlikely that I will go to you and check it out, since often such reports are conveyed in confidence. Yet even if I don't believe the report, it has planted a seed of suspicion in my mind about you. As Deborah Tannen reported about a Washington *Post* article she read: "Rumors are effective even if they are later disproved and retracted; the damage is done by their mere existence, because most people assume 'where there's smoke, there's fire.'"[3]

Second, while it's both sinisterly flattering and enchanting to have someone take me into their confidence and then divulge some bit of secret gossip about someone else, Deborah Tannen is right with her observation that "it is natural to assume that someone who has only negative things to say about others will also say negative things about you when you aren't there."[4]

Can you see how such reports become the great climate buster, shattering the safe environment Jesus ordained the church to be, and creating instead a climate of suspicion and mistrust within the church? The same principle holds true, of course, within families and workplaces.

And yet, in my observation, this is happening without impunity throughout the church, from the highest levels of leadership on down to the members in the pew. We will labor long with members caught smoking, and discipline them if they continue, but not so with members who decimate the safe climate of the church by wholesale violation of Jesus' commandment on how to approach others. Nor do I mean to convey that I have this commandment mastered within my own life. It's a very hard commandment for me. I have to go before my congregation rather frequently and ask them to check me if I begin to give an evil report behind someone's back. I ask each member of our congregation to covenant with each other not to violate Jesus' commandment for building a safe, nurturing climate in the church.

How to Go

If I determine that I need to go to you and talk with you personally about a matter of this nature, how should I do it?

First, I need to prayerfully consider Jesus' words: "Why do you see the speck in your neighbor's eye, but do not notice the log in your own eye? Or how can you say to your neighbor, 'Let me take the speck out of your eye,' while the log is in your own eye? You hypocrite, first take the log out of your own eye, and then you will see clearly to take the speck out of your neighbor's eye" (Matt. 7:3-5, NRSV).

Ellen White likewise cautions: "Do not set yourself up as a standard. Do not make your opinions, your views of duty, your interpretations of Scripture, a criterion for others and in your heart condemn them if they do not come up to your ideal."[5] "Christlike love places the most favorable construction on the motives and acts of others."[6]

It may seem at first that such admonitions should stop me in my tracks and keep me from ever speaking to you about the offense I've observed in you or the hurt you've inflicted on me. But that's not at all what Jesus intended. He wants the occasion to result in spiritual growth in me, and to provide the same opportunity for you. Before I draw close to you, to discuss the matter with you, He wants me to draw closer to Him. He wants me to pray to be imbued with the spirit of Galatians 6:1: "Brothers, if someone is caught in a sin, you who are spiritual should restore him gently. But watch yourself, or you also may be tempted." When I finally approach you, I do not do it as an angel confronting a sinner, but as one recovering sinner to another.

Sometimes a member will phone me and describe an offense, using no names, seeking counsel as to how to apply this first step in that situation. I consider such inquiries appropriate, because the individual is making no attempt to hurt anyone or depreciate him or her behind his or her back, but rather to determine how to safeguard the other person's reputation and effectively achieve resolution and reconciliation.

I've discovered that in most cases, disputes and injuries of a personal nature resolve themselves when the two individuals involved prayerfully discuss the matter alone, between the two of them. Jesus knew, of course, that it would be that way.

Level Two: Take Another With You

But if you and your offender cannot work out the issue alone, then you need to determine if it is important enough to escalate to level two of the commandment. Upon prayerful reflection, you may determine that prayer and time will likely enable you to heal from your wound without taking further steps. You may conclude that the sin you observed in the person may not, after all, threaten his or her spiritual relationship in the way you once thought.

But if you consider it to be more serious than that, then it should be carefully and prayerfully escalated to the next level of intervention: *"Take one or two others along with you, so that every word may be confirmed by the evidence of two or three witnesses"* (Matt. 18:16, NRSV).

It is at this point, it seems to me, that it might be appropriate to seek the services of a Christian counselor in those cases in which husband/wife, parent/child, or other interpersonal conflicts can't be resolved between the individual parties involved.

By escalating the matter to involve one or two others, Jesus is still trying to keep it in the smallest circle of influence possible for the protection of the reputations of the people involved. At no point along the way does Jesus authorize me to talk about you behind your back. The intent is that you will be present when I tell my story to the third party.

Christ's provision does not authorize me to go out and pick one or two of my best friends whom I believe will see things my way. It's best to have both parties choose one or two members of the church that they both respect and have confidence in.

This step accesses the unbiased judgment of mutually agreed upon third parties to help bring resolution to the conflict and reconciliation between members. The third party may even perceive that the offense I'm accusing you of is more my problem than yours. When I go into this step, I need to have a humble, teachable attitude and be willing to change myself if need be.

Such situations demand the most fervent prayer. And this is the context for Jesus' well-known promise: "If two of you on earth agree about anything you ask for, it will be done for you by my Father in heaven. For where two or three come together in my name, there am I with them" (verses 19, 20).

I have witnessed some tearful reconciliations at this level of intervention. Unfortunately, however, it doesn't always turn out so favorably. And if reconciliation fails at this stage, then Jesus says: *"Tell it to the church; and if the offender refuses to listen even to the church, let such a one be to you as a Gentile and a tax collector"* (verse 17, NRSV).

Level Three: Tell It to the Church

Level three invites the members of the church to unite in prayer and loving entreaty that the offender may yet be restored. God may have an expanded purpose in allowing the problem to be exposed to the whole church. It may be that others in the church are also dealing with similar problems. Thus level three intervention is a divine call for individuals throughout the congregation to search their hearts, confess their sins, and seek divine cleansing. A deepening of congregational spirituality may ensue.

What if the member being counseled refuses the united appeals of the church? Such ones may have demonstrated by their own actions that they have severed themselves from the church, and an official action of the church to disfellowship may be the appropriate response.

When a congregation administers such severe discipline, it must not only continue to pray and work for the spiritual restoration of the disciplined member, but may also appropriately pray a prayer of repentance for any misjudgment or unnecessary harshness it may have exercised in the administration of the discipline. Such a prayer may be modeled after one written by Jim Kok, chaplain at Pine Rest Christian Hospital, Grand Rapids, Michigan, upon the firing of a young teacher over a problem that developed during the school year:

"Lord, we have just decided on taking a lady out of her classroom, away from her students forever. . . . We hurt for her as we do this. We cry for her pupils who will miss her. We ache because her colleagues will miss her too. We believe this is the right thing to do.

We trust that You led us to this choice. We want to do what is right for the Christian community, for the school, for the lives of the children. But we can't do it without hurting people. People may even be turned away from You because of this. She, whose services we are terminating, will be injured deeply at a time when she needs support and encouragement from the Christian community. O Lord, we hate being put in this position, hurting people and even giving people reason to question You. But we do believe it is right. Nevertheless, Lord, in the corners of our hearts there is also the haunting fear that we could be wrong. As we understand things, we don't think so. But we could be wrong. And we beg Your forgiveness if out of the limitations of our human condition we have been mistaken. Accept our efforts, Lord. We hesitatingly present our decision and stand behind it. Heal, comfort, sustain those whom we've hurt in doing what we believe is Your will. . . . Support and encourage us who have to do this awful deed. Amen."[7]

Paul adds in 2 Thessalonians 3:15: "Count [such a one] not as an enemy, but admonish him as a brother" (KJV). And in 2 Corinthians 2:6-8, he adds: "The punishment inflicted on him by the majority is sufficient for him. Now instead, you ought to forgive and comfort him, so that he will not be overwhelmed by excessive sorrow. I urge you, therefore, to reaffirm your love for him."

Because even at the end of the process, God still seeks to restore His wandering child. He still leaves the ninety and nine to go after the one who is not in the fold, to reclaim him or her, to heal and restore that person to His fold again. His heart aches with divine restlessness until the individual is back.

---

[1] E. G. White, *Testimonies,* vol. 5, pp. 616, 617.

[2] *Ibid.,* vol. 2, p. 54.

[3] Deborah Tannen, *You Just Don't Understand: Women and Men in Conversation* (New York: Ballantine Books, 1990), p. 106.

[4] *Ibid.,* p. 120.

[5] E. G. White, *Thoughts From the Mount of Blessing* (Mountain View, Calif.: Pacific Press Pub. Assn., 1956), p. 124.

[6] ———— , *The Acts of the Apostles* (Mountain View, Calif.: Pacific Press Pub. Assn., 1911), p. 319.

[7] Jim Kok, quoted in Arnold Kurtz, "A Day of Mourning," *Ministry,* May 1982, p. 12.

CHAPTER SEVEN

How to Go to Church With Someone You Don't Agree With

The ordinary Adventist today sits just down the pew from other members whose theological viewpoints and lifestyles differ somewhat from his own. The church doesn't seek to hide these differences, but rather seems to even encourage healthy debate. In 1975 the Southern Publishing Association published *Perfection,* a book that presented four differing viewpoints on what constitutes Christian perfection, authored by four Adventist scholars who held those views. The June 1985 issue of *Ministry,* the professional journal for Adventist ministers, carried two major articles on the nature of Christ's humanity, one defending "sinless nature," the other supporting "sinful nature," with an accompanying editorial appealing for continued study and cautioning against extreme rigidity of positions on the subject.

Another case in point is Martin Weber's 1991 best-seller, *Adventist Hot Potatoes,* which sold 24,000 copies in its first six months. Published by the Pacific Press Publishing Association, Weber's book discussed a whole series of hotly contested issues in the church today, including celebration-style worship, church discipline, and whether someone wearing a wedding ring should hold church office. In his 1992 sequel, *More Adventist Hot Potatoes,* Weber took his own position on the nature of Christ, among other subjects.

The ordinary Adventist today belongs to a congregation that has loyal members who take opposite points of view on almost every one of these issues. Whenever a congregation is "blessed" by such diversity, the potential exists for misunderstanding, accusation, and division, but also for growth in learning to love. It all depends on how it's approached.

How can you go to church and thrive in a congregation of such varied viewpoints and lifestyles?

The Central Focus

The viewpoints of Jesus' disciples differed significantly from each other on many things. But Jesus pointed them to a more central focus that transcended their differences: "By this everyone will know that you are my disciples, if you have love for one another" (John 13:35, NRSV). I take this to mean that within my congregation with its many differences I can serve Jesus best by seeking to come into a unity with my brothers and sisters through the acceptance of Christian love.

Note the way Ellen White expressed this sentiment: "The powers of darkness stand a poor chance against believers who love one another as Christ has loved them, who refuse to create alienation and strife, who stand together, who are kind, courteous, and tenderhearted, cherishing the faith that works by love and purifies the soul."[1] "The strength of God's people lies in their union with Him through His only-begotten Son, and their union with one another."[2]

Such a unity, however, does not necessarily mean that we understand everything in exactly the same way. Note how the statement just quoted continues: "There are no two leaves of a tree precisely alike; neither do all minds run in the same direction [i.e., we will have different viewpoints; that's a given]. But while this is so, there may be unity in diversity."[3] "Harmony and union existing among men of varied dispositions is the strongest witness that can be borne that God has sent His Son into the world to save sinners."[4]

How can we achieve such unity? "The closer our union with Christ, the closer will be our union with one another."[5] Evidently, as I approach Jesus through an active devotional experience and a life of service, I will not merely learn to tolerate fellow members who differ from me, I will actually learn to respect and appreciate them, and to grow through my interaction with them. And I can honestly say that I have experienced this. Not in every case, maybe, but to a significant extent. It's a process of growth.

I realize, of course, that we can carry the unity-in-diversity theme only so far. It didn't keep Luther tethered to the Catholic Church indefinitely. Seventh-day Adventists resist the premise of the modern ecumenical movement that we should be willing to sacrifice deeply held core beliefs for the sake of unity at all costs. We wouldn't dream of trying to stretch the unity-in-diversity theme to attempt unity with a satanist group. Common sense limits the application. But the Adventist faith has fairly wide boundary lines within which we can speak of unity in diversity. I will get to those boundary lines in a moment.

Diversity—A Treasure

I believe we should thank God for our diversity. It's a beautiful thing.

But in Philippians 2:2 Paul appealed for believers to be "like-minded." How can we be thankful for diversity within the church when we are supposed to be "like-minded"? Just what did Paul mean by his invitation "Make my joy complete by being like-minded"? Did he intend for us to think exactly alike in every respect? If so, then whose mind among us is the standard for all the others to conform to? I'd vote for it to be my mind, you understand. But that would probably be the only vote my mind would get. Is not Paul, rather, appealing for us to be like-minded with the mind of Christ? Yes, for in that same passage he speaks of "being united with Christ, . . . having the same love, being one in spirit and purpose" (Phil. 2:1, 2).

If unity means uniformity of thought and lifestyle, then the Jehovah's Witnesses surely have it. I've written two books on their beliefs, and I can testify that they allow no room for discussion of beliefs or variance of lifestyle within their system. I don't mean to demean the rank-and-file Jehovah's Witness member. They have some very beautiful, godly people among them. But the system itself is one of rigid mind control, in my estimation. Studying their beliefs as I did made me appreciate the Adventist faith even more. Not just the Adventist beliefs only, but the freedom of thought and practice that we allow within our church. I thank God for it. Such freedom is not without its problems. But that was true in heaven, too, wasn't it? Evidently God considered such freedom to be worth the risks.

Alden Thompson's book *Inspiration,* published in 1991 by the

Review and Herald, was a great blessing to many Seventh-day Adventists. But not to all. The Adventist Theological Society shortly countered with a publication of their own, warning that in their opinion some of Thompson's premises were on shaky ground. Thompson then came to the Seventh-day Adventist Seminary in Berrien Springs and interacted in a public discussion with professors who questioned certain tenets of his position. The exchange was frank, but a wholesome spirit prevailed. I'm proud to belong to a church like that.

The worldwide Adventist community has awakened to the dawn of a new day with respect to the role of women in the church. Perhaps "reawakened" would be a more appropriate term, if we understand our Adventist history aright. Local churches throughout North America debate the pros and cons of ordaining women to the ministry of local church elder. Each congregation has the right to make its own decision based on the understanding and readiness of its own membership. All the while the debate goes on at higher levels about the appropriateness of the ordination of women to the gospel ministry. The strain of the debate appears at all levels of the church, including the local churches in which we worship, as the Spirit patiently reveals His mind through the dawning awareness of His people. The debate is excruciatingly uncomfortable at times, and in some cases seriously strains relationships between local church members who hold differing views. And the process seems so painstakingly slow for some of us. But I so much appreciate the climate of freedom in which the process takes place.

It would be so much easier for me if everyone thought as I do about such issues. And you'd have to admit that it would be more comfortable for you if we all shared your viewpoints and did things just the way you think they should be done. But we'd all miss so much if it were that way. Our diversity represents a beautiful richness and strength. As uncomfortable as it can be for me sometimes, I thank God for it. It gives us the opportunity to learn the discipline of love in treating others who disagree with us the same as we want to be treated when we disagree with them.

Where to Draw the Line

But now for the hard part. How far can I wander out into left field or right field without leaving the ballpark? At what point does diversity in viewpoint become heresy, and diversity in lifestyle become apostasy?

If this decision were left up to me, you'd be a heretic and apostate in those areas where you strongly disagree with me. And I suppose that if you made the decisions, I'd be the one in trouble. I'm thankful that neither is the case.

The boundaries of acceptable diversity is best left to church leaders who have been ordained and empowered to make such decisions. I don't know any other way it could work in a denomination our size. It's for sure that I'm not a safe one to set those boundary lines for you, and I wouldn't want you deciding them for me. But somebody has to establish them.

By and large, that's what the *Seventh-day Adventist Church Manual* does. The *Church Manual* can be revised only at a General Conference session. So it has widespread denominational input. I know that it's always possible for politics to somehow get injected, but I don't know a better way to determine and draw boundaries.

The *Church Manual* sets forth the fundamental beliefs of the church as well as the core lifestyle issues involved in being a Seventh-day Adventist. On the one hand, our church cannot afford to lose our historical, Bible-based identity as the distinctive witness to the world that God called us to be through the prayerful study and deliberations of our pioneers. On the other hand, Adventists have historically resisted establishing a formalized creed that refuses to respond to the continual leading of the Holy Spirit, who never ceases shaping the unchanging eternal realities of Scripture into a present truth for each new generation. Both powerful themes weave through the preamble to the Fundamental Beliefs of Seventh-day Adventists that expresses the historically preserving, yet ever questing dynamic of the Seventh-day Adventist movement: "Seventh-day Adventists accept the Bible as their only creed and hold certain fundamental beliefs to be the teaching of the Holy Scriptures. These beliefs, as set forth here, constitute the church's understanding and expression of the teaching of Scripture. Revision of these statements may be expected at a General Conference session when the church is led by the Holy Spirit to a fuller understanding of Bible truth or finds better language in which to express the teachings of God's Holy Word. [A statement of the 27 fundamental beliefs of the church follows.]"[6]

We have some latitude in how we may understand and express some of these things. But basically, the *Church Manual* is the safest guide we have as to what the boundaries are for acceptable diversity.

The Theological/Lifestyle "Demilitarized Zone"

I think of this defined range of acceptable diversity as the Adventist theological and lifestyle demilitarized zone. And I've come to the conclusion that within those boundaries, the greater the honest differences and respectful discussion among us, the greater the potential for deepening our understanding, for learning to love, and for developing Christian character. It might also be considered the unity-in-diversity zone, a crucible of sorts for the continual development and growth of accepting love.

Local churches and conferences must apply these guidelines, through much prayer and discussion, to their own settings. It is incumbent upon denominational leaders at higher levels to determine when wider subgroups within the church have crossed over the line of acceptable diversity. When you read the North American Division document *Issues,* which identifies several independent ministries that had crossed over the line of acceptable diversity within the church, you can see how church leaders struggle long and agonizingly over such determinations. The process is not foolproof. Mistakes get made, because it's still people who make the decisions. But it's the best we have, and I'm thankful for it.

At the local congregation level, someone stepping over the line of acceptable diversity does not necessarily mean that the congregation should remove him or her from church membership. Through prayer and personal work the church can often reclaim such individuals. But even when they can't, the decision the church should make is not always easy. In Jesus' parable of the wheat and the tares, He instructed the disciples that they were not to throw the tares out until the harvest, by which He meant when He would return at the end of the world (Matt. 13:24-30, 36-43). Commenting on this, Ellen White warned: "As the tares have their roots closely intertwined with those of the good grain, so false brethren in the church may be closely linked with true disciples. The real character of these pretended believers is not fully manifested. Were they to be separated from the church, others might be caused to stumble, who but for this would have remained steadfast."[7]

Accept Other Members as Being as Sincere as . . .

The gospel makes possible a wonderful freedom to accept each member of your congregation as being as sincere in his or her relationship with God as you are seeking to be in yours.

As I became acquainted with the members of my first church in Winnemucca, Nevada, I observed some things that made me suspicious that some of them were not genuine Christians. I wondered if our church could grow under such circumstances. So I confided in my conference president, the late Dan E. Dirksen, a real saint. He said, "Skip, I learned something a long time ago that has been a great blessing to me ever since. I learned to accept every member of my congregation as being as sincere in their relationship with God as I was trying to be in mine. Don't be constantly trying to determine which members of your congregation are genuine Christians and which aren't. Love them and serve them, and leave the results with God."

When I heard that, I began to doubt Dirksen's experience! But the Holy Spirit didn't give up on me, and eventually I began to enjoy the freedom that Dirksen spoke of.

Jesus invited us to this freedom when He said, "Do not judge, or you too will be judged" (Matt. 7:1), and "whoever is not against us is for us" (Mark 9:40). Note in the following two statements how Ellen White expresses this freedom—first, regarding differing viewpoints: "Do not set yourselves up as a standard. Do not make your opinions, your views of duty, your interpretations of Scripture, a criterion for others, and in your heart condemn them if they do not come up to your ideal."[8] Then regarding differing lifestyles: "Christlike love places the most favorable construction on the motives and acts of others."[9]

Dirksen was right! I really can enjoy the freedom of accepting other members in my church as being as sincere in their relationship with God as I am seeking to be in mine.

How to Relate to the Tares

Does this mean I become a spiritual ostrich, with my head stuck in the sand of illusory belief that the church contains no unconverted people? No. Jesus told us plainly that the enemy has sown tares among the wheat (Matt. 13:25). But we've also been given this revelation: "The Lord does not look at the things man looks at.

Man looks at the outward appearance, but the Lord looks at the heart" (1 Sam. 16:7). I take this to mean that I can't trust my judgment about who in the church are genuine in their relationship with God, and who are not. Only the Lord Himself knows a person's true inner nature, and I best leave that judgment with Him.

But even if it were possible for me to discern the tares from the wheat, that wouldn't mean I should necessarily treat them differently. Jesus dealt with Judas the same as the other disciples. Minutes before Judas betrayed Him, Jesus washed Judas' feet and protected his identity as the betrayer, leaving us an example of the climate He would have prevail in the church (John 13:12-15, 18-29). He treated the tares just as He would want to be treated were He in their place.

In such a climate, and within the bounds of the church's defined theological and lifestyle demilitarized zone, or unity-in-diversity zone, members who differ can grow in accepting love through respectful interaction with one another. Such a climate answers the heartfelt, plaintive queries of a poem I came across recently:

> "If this is not a place where tears are understood,
>   Where do I go to cry?
> If this is not a place where my spirit can take wing,
>   Where do I go to fly?
> If this is not a place where my questions can be asked,
>   Where do I go to seek?
> If this is not a place where my feelings can be heard,
>   Where do I go to speak?
> If this is not a place where you'll accept me as I am,
>   Where do I go to be?
> If this is not a place where I can try, and learn, and grow,
>   Where can I just be me?"

—Author Unknown

Where the Rubber Meets the Road

In a church I once served, the head elder and I held opposite views on whether or not someone wearing a wedding band should be allowed to hold a church office. What made it so serious was that shortly before I came to the church, the nominating committee filled several church offices with members who wore wedding bands. When the church board found out what happened, they held an emergency board meeting and instructed the nominating committee not to fill any office with someone who chose to keep wearing a wedding band. Several of the young adults involved threatened to leave the church. That's when I arrived.

The head elder and I had some heated discussions over this issue. He told me that he seriously questioned the Christian experience of members who disagreed with his position. In fact, he felt so deeply about this that he said he wasn't sure he could remain a member of a congregation who chose to disregard what he felt was the spiritual principle involved. That gave me an opportunity to share with him what Dan Dirksen had taught me several years earlier. After that, I think my head elder questioned my experience!

We agreed to have a business meeting and debate it before the whole church. Practically the entire congregation showed up. At the end of his presentation, the head elder said, "I just want to say two more things." I thought, *Oh boy, here it comes.* "I just want everyone here tonight to know," he went on, "that I do not question the Christian experience of those who see this differently, and if the vote goes the other way, I will support it."

Yes! I thought to myself.

The vote went against my position, but that didn't matter. The climate was being created for some good things to happen in that church. And they did. The head elder and I went together to the homes of the young adults involved, to talk to them and pray with them. We didn't lose one of them. And the head elder and I went on to become the very best of friends.

I love the diversity of our church, and I love the freedom Jesus gave us to accept and love every member in it.

---

[1] E. G. White, *Our Father Cares,* p. 36.

[2] *The SDA Bible Commentary,* Ellen G. White Comments, vol. 6, p. 1083.

[3] *Ibid.*

[4] ———, *Testimonies,* vol. 8, p. 242.

[5] ———, *Our Father Cares,* p. 36.

[6] *Seventh-day Adventist Church Manual,* 15th ed. (Hagerstown, Md.: Review and Herald Pub. Assn., 1995), pp. 7-17.

[7] E. G. White, *Christ's Object Lessons* (Washington, D.C.: Review and Herald Pub. Assn., 1900), p. 72.

[8] ———, *Thoughts From the Mount of Blessing,* p. 124.

[9] ———, *The Acts of the Apostles,* p. 319.

CHAPTER EIGHT

Good Adventists Don't Have Problems at Home, Do They?

Suppose you were serving on your church's nominating committee considering names for a major church office and someone recommended a member you knew was having severe problems at home—perhaps marital estrangement, or financial embarrassment, or parent-teenager fallout, etc. Maybe you had even heard that the nominee had been admitted to a psychiatric ward a couple years earlier. Would you consider such an individual qualified to hold a major office in your church? Would you consider him or her to be a good Adventist?

How could a good Adventist have financial problems in light of God's promise to bless and protect abundantly those who return a faithful tithe to Him? (See Mal. 3:10-12.) How could you be a good Adventist and end up in a psychiatric ward when Philippians 4:6, 7 assures that if you take all of your anxieties to God in prayer, "the peace of God, which transcends all understanding, will guard your hearts and your minds in Christ Jesus"? How can good Adventists become estranged from their spouses, considering Solomon's observation: "When the ways of people please the Lord, he causes even their enemies to be at peace with them" (Prov. 16:7, NRSV)? How could a good Adventist who truly loves the Lord get a divorce in light of such texts as Malachi 2:16: " 'I hate divorce,' says the Lord God of Israel"? How could good Adventist parents have their children turn out bad when Proverbs 22:6 assures, "Train a child in the way he should go, and when he is old he will not turn from it"? Based on such straight-forward texts, Paul instructed that anyone considered for a major church office "must manage his own household well, keeping his children submissive and respectful in every way—for if someone does not know how to manage his own household, how can he take care of God's church?" (1 Tim. 3:4, 5, NRSV).

The Messiest Divorce Ever

Let me tell you the story of perhaps the messiest divorce on record. Having had to do some sleuthing to find out about it, I wish I didn't have to tell it. But it illustrates an important point.

The source I got this story from couldn't remember when Luci and Theo weren't together. It seemed to be love at first sight. Everybody who knew them considered them the perfect couple. They adored each other. My source swears they never spoke an un-kind word to each other before the change came. One man I shared this story with said, "That was their problem—they were denying their differences. They should have had some good healthy argu-ments along the way." But of course, he hadn't heard the whole story yet, so we can forgive him for his hasty conclusion.

Theo and Luci lived before our day of small families. There were nine children. They seemed to do everything right and spent lots of quality time together. Never missing family worship, they went to church together every Sabbath. As I later studied the report of this story for myself, I honestly didn't know what Luci and Theo could have done differently to secure their marriage and family.

No one I've consulted on this story has ventured a single credi-ble clue as to how the estrangement started. From what I've been able to gather, one day Theo just noticed that Luci was acting dif-ferently than usual. To this day, no one suspects that there was any third party involved. Theo did notice, however, that Luci was spend-ing increasing amounts of time in front of the mirror, primping.

As soon as Theo noticed the slightest hint of a change in Luci's attitude toward him, he began to talk to her about it. That was the beginning of an unbelievable nightmare for Theo. At first Luci seemed to want to work things out. But those times didn't last long. The relationship deteriorated rapidly. Eventually Luci drew the children into the conflict, attempting to convince them that Dad's household rules were overbearing, making him guilty of mental and emotional abuse. She longed to escape what she considered Theo's dominant control of her and the children.

According to court records, it was Theo who finally filed for divorce. If you don't think that sent shock waves through the church. One source I consulted surmised that Theo waited until no doubt remained that Luci had already divorced him in her own heart. In fact, one person told me that she marveled at Theo's patience, but wondered in retrospect if he may not have waited too long given the damaging influence Luci apparently had on some of the children while she remained at home.

It wasn't what you'd call one of those "clean" divorces in which the parties somehow manage to remain friends through it all. The court proceeding was excruciatingly painful for both. The children were old enough to choose where they wanted to go. Three of them decided to live with Luci. Losing those children tore Theo's heart out. Luci had so turned them against their father that they never wanted to see him again.

Eventually, Luci threw off all pretenses of being a Christian. She became increasingly bitter as the years passed. When Theo went on with his life and increased his family, Luci turned on his new children with a vengeance. And the story isn't over yet.

I'm sure by now that you recognize the story of the great divorce between *Luci*fer and *Theo*s (the Greek term for "God"). Of course, it's not accurate in every detail. For one thing, I did not intend to suggest that God is male and Lucifer female. Genesis 1:27 suggests that God has both male and female qualities. And as for Lucifer? Well, who knows? Nor did the children (angels) belong to both God and Lucifer, for God created them all, including the angel Lucifer himself. And there were more like 9 trillion children involved, give or take a few trillion.

But on the whole the story is surprisingly, if not uncomfortably, accurate. Enough so to challenge simplistic conclusions about people who go through serious personal and family problems.

Someone might question whether it's legitimate to portray Lucifer and God in a spousal relationship. Lucifer was the "guardian cherub" "on the holy mount of God," and as such stood in a closer relation to God than any other of the angelic family (Eze. 28:14). Their relationship started out perfect, but eventually, through the indulgence of pride, Lucifer turned against God, desired control of the angelic family, caused intense strife among them, and was ultimately cast out (divorced, with a restraining order that prevented him from returning home) (Eze. 28:15-17; Rev. 12:7-9). One third of God's angelic children choose to leave home with Lucifer and never return (Rev. 12:3, 4, 9). When God said, "I hate divorce," He was speaking from personal experience (Mal. 2:16). If it still seems too irreverent to refer to God as a husband who would divorce His spouse, consider God's own testimony as Israel's self-proclaimed "husband": "I gave faithless Israel her certificate of divorce and sent her away because of all her adulteries" (Isa. 54:5; Jer. 3:8).

How It Could Happen

How could such a thing happen in a family that was so close, that never missed family worship, that did everything right? What did God do wrong as a husband that caused Him to lose the one closest to Him? If God can make the enemies of those who please Him live at peace with them (Prov. 16:7), why couldn't He make His own enemies be at peace with Himself? If children who are trained up right do not depart from the faith when they are grown (Prov. 22:6), then what did God do wrong in the way He trained the angels? Would the fact that God went through divorce and lost a third of His own children disqualify Him from serving in a church office that Paul said should be filled only by someone who proved he could manage his family well (1 Tim. 3:15)?

Ellen White once wrote, "God wants us all to have common sense, and He wants us to reason from common sense."[1] The story of what happened to God's own family gives us a basis for applying some of the biblical admonitions and promises in a realistic way.

There's one factor that even God Himself has to deal with and that makes all the promises conditional to a certain extent—God's own wonderful gift of *free choice*. We know immediately that Lucifer's, and the fallen angels', abuse of that gift explains God's divorce and why some of His own children ran away from home permanently. But we have a hard time giving each other the same benefit of the doubt.

The Main Cause of Our Problems at Home

In one respect—a big one—we're justified in being so hard on ourselves and on each other when such problems happen to us. After all, we're sinners, while God is perfect. "Sinners" isn't merely a religious label we wear. As sinners who actually commit sin, we act selfishly to get what we want, irrespective of the needs of others or the damage it may cause them. In so doing, we offend people and hurt them. We sin as spouses. We sin as parents. We sin as children. Our sinning sometimes causes wounds so deep that those we've injured must move away from us to ensure their own survival. Wherever there are relationship estrangements, our own sinfulness is the first thing that we should rightfully suspect as the cause.

Sin—as our failure to trust our lives and welfare completely into the hands of God, our selfish behavior, our willful disregard of God's commandments, our irresponsible stewardship patterns of compulsive spending or careless financial management, etc.—may cause all of the problems we have discussed in this chapter.

But Don't Forget the Innocent

Sin is not the only reason for every problem we encounter. Of course, if there were no sin at all, the problems we are discussing here would not exist. But what I mean is that what we all know to be perfectly true in God's case—He did not sin, and yet He had problems—may also be true for others.

Job is a case in point. He was, of course, a sinner. But the Bible makes clear that his suffering had no direct connection to his own sin. He was an innocent sufferer. In fact, it was his integrity that brought on his suffering. Paul is another example. His unflinching obedience to God brought him much suffering (2 Cor. 11:23-29).

The author of Psalm 44 complained to God for abandoning His people to their enemies even though "we had not forgotten you or been false to your covenant. . . . For your sake we face death all day long; we are considered as sheep to be slaughtered" (verses 17-22). For a long time I felt very uncomfortable with this strong declaration of one's innocence in the face of severe problems. But I've come to accept it as additional inspired evidence that innocent people do indeed suffer.

Jesus Himself warned that an uncompromising commitment to follow Him will bring a sword into some families and workplaces, causing severe estrangements (Matt. 10:34-39; Luke 12:49-53; 14:25-33). In these same passages He even said that anyone not willing to pay such a price for the kingdom's sake is not worthy of Him.

The point is, when someone in the church experiences family, physical or mental health, or financial problems, we cannot always know if their sin caused it, or if they are for the most part innocent victims. God alone knows the full circumstances, and the issues of the heart in these matters. And Jesus has instructed us not even to try to judge such matters, lest we be guilty of arriving at the wrong conclusion (Matt. 7:1-3).

If You Are Having Problems at Home

1. Seize the Opportunity for Spiritual Development
View personal and relationship problems as opportunities for growth. Pray with David, "Search me, O God, and know my heart; test me and know my anxious thoughts. See if there is any offensive way in me, and lead me in the way everlasting" (Ps. 139:23, 24). That is a healthy prayer. It is also safe, for the Lord will only reveal to you those areas of need that you are ready to grow in by His grace. Repenting for the ways you may have contributed to your problems opens the door for God to free you from repeating those same mistakes again and again to your own detriment. "If we confess our sins, he is faithful and just and will forgive us our sins and purify us from all unrighteousness" (1 John 1:9).

Having problems at home can make you feel very unspiritual, since you may conclude that if you had been a perfect Christian all along, you may have been spared from the problems you now have. But if you will seize the present moment and seek God's help, He can create a pure heart in you and renew a right spirit within you (Ps. 51:10).

Whether your problems are the result of your own sins and mistakes, or whether you are an innocent sufferer, or more likely still, some combination of the two, you have God's sure promise: "In all things God works for the good of those who love him" (Rom. 8:28). No matter how hopeless and unresolvable your problems may appear, if you will hold fast to God and rely upon Him He will employ His divine artistry to bring something good out of your situation.

Portraying God as a master sculptor, Rick Rice illustrates God's ability to work creatively with our worst problems and mistakes to make them appear actually to enhance His original design for our lives:

"Imagine a sculptor at work on a block of marble. He has made careful calculations and taken precise measurements. With hammer and chisel he seeks to free the figure he has designed from the stone surrounding it. Now suppose, after the project is well under way, he uncovers a streak of discoloration running through the block, making it impossible for him to fulfill his original design. What should he do?

"One alternative, of course, would be to get rid of the block and find another without flaws. But suppose the sculptor has an attachment to this particular piece of stone. There are qualities in it that he values and wants to display. So instead of discarding the material, he changes his original design; he alters his work to fit the new situation.

"Let us further imagine that in the final product, the overall design is so perfectly adapted to the flaw in the marble, that instead of detracting from the beauty of the work, it actually enhances it. The sculptor looks for all the world as if the artist planned for the discoloration from the very beginning."[2]

2. Go for Help

It's a tragedy that so many ordinary Adventists consider it an admission of weakness to seek help when they encounter major problems. I know all the arguments against going for aid—I've used them myself. "I should be able to just pray about it and *handle it myself*" are famous last words for too many marriages, too many parent/child relationships, too many members sliding toward depression, too many financial entanglements.

Does the suggestion to go for help depreciate in some way the value of prayer? By no means. When we encounter major problems, we ought to pray more than ever. But when prayer alone does not resolve the matter, it just makes sense to seek supplementary aid.

I'm convinced that our traditional understanding of Jesus' invitation "Ask and it will be given to you" (Matt. 7:7) has a blind side to it. Without doubt, Jesus meant this to be first understood in its vertical application: *"Ask God,* and He will give unto you." But that is not literally what He said. He simply said, "Ask." I believe He did so because He intended for there also to be a horizontal dimension to the asking—*"Ask each other,* and it shall be given unto you." First, ask God for help, but then be open as well to the ministry of others.

Of course, such "others" should be competent, godly people (Ps. 1:1)—a Christian friend, perhaps, or your pastor, or a Christian counselor, or even some good books on the subject. You may need the emergency, round-the-clock care that can be provided only in a hospital setting, or by staying with another family for a while.

If yours is a relationship problem, don't conclude that your spouse, or child, etc., must seek help with you in order for the relationship to improve. In her excellent book *Divorce Busting: A Revolutionary and Rapid Program for "Staying Together"* Michele Weiner-Davis says, "I have observed hundreds of people change their relationships without the presence of their spouse in therapy and without a formal agreement from their spouse to work on the marriage."[3] The important thing is to get help before things deteriorate to a crisis point, if at all possible.

To seek the aid you need is not a sign of weakness—it's just the opposite. If you ever feel embarrassed for wanting help, remember Jesus' statement: "Blessed are the poor in spirit, for theirs is the kingdom of heaven" (Matt. 5:3). That may seem like a tame, innocuous statement to us, but it was a bombshell to those who first heard it. It was the opening salvo of Jesus' inaugural address, the Sermon on the Mount. In His audience that day were the wealthy, the educated, the beautiful people, the position holders, the self-assured, self-made achievers, all hoping to be commended for their independence and drafted into the Miracle Worker's new government. But His opening words set an entirely different tone. They affirmed "the poor in spirit"—those struggling with chronic and seemingly insurmountable problems, who knew they'd come to the end of their own resources, and were seeking help. When you search for the help you need, you have Jesus' approval.

If You Know Someone Who's Having Problems at Home

When you become aware of members struggling with homelife problems, resist the inclination to try to determine to what extent their problems are self-induced (Matt. 7:1-3). They may be innocent sufferers. If so, they deserve all the support we can possibly give to help them withstand the assault of the enemy. Even if their problems may be entirely of their own making, we can offer them the same forgiveness Jesus offered to us while we were still His enemies (Rom. 5:6-8).

Paul said, "If one member suffers, all suffer together with it" (1 Cor. 12:26, NRSV). Jesus instructed us to treat fellow members who are having problems at home as we ourselves would want to be dealt with if we were in their place (Matt. 7:12). Applying this radical requirement of love may stretch us beyond our present ability to identify and adapt, but this is love's true dynamic and adventure. Rather than ignore, isolate, or shun fellow members in trouble, we've been set free to accept and support them in every way we can. "To take people right where they are, whatever their position or condition, and help them in every way possible—this is gospel ministry."[4] That may mean simply listening to them, or affirming them for taking the difficult step of seeking outside help, or calling to see how they're doing, or offering to watch their children one night a month for a few months, or even inviting them to stay in our homes for a couple days when they are in crisis. The Holy Spirit will teach you how to make the appropriate application.

Any church that becomes this kind of supportive, caring community for members who hurt will be a powerful witness in their community. "If we would humble ourselves before God, and be kind and courteous and tenderhearted and pitiful (emphatic), there would be one hundred conversions to the truth where now there is only one."[5] Such a church tends also to hold on to those it wins.

Self-disclosure

It wasn't easy for God to tell the story of His divorce. He hinted about it in little bits and pieces, "at many times and in various ways" (Heb. 1:1). But not until the Bible was nearly completed, in the middle of the book of Revelation, did God actually talk about the divorce itself. He may have wanted to tell us sooner, but perhaps we weren't ready. "There was war in heaven" is the way John put it (Rev. 12:7). It makes me feel good about Him that He would finally share it with us.

Remember that it's never easy to speak of something as painful as that. One relives a lot in the process. But sometimes it can help someone else. With that in mind, but with considerable reluctance, I must tell you some of my own story.

In 1979 my wife of 13 years felt she had to leave. She moved a thousand miles away, taking with her our three sons, who ranged in ages from 7 to 1½ years. At first I felt innocent. But with the passing of months and years God taught me my own responsibility in the breakup of the marriage. That awareness and admission was essential for me to experience growth.

My local church did exactly the right thing for me. They accepted me and asked me to stay. Several offered to let me live with them at the peak of the crisis when they felt I needed extra support. At times I would come home at night to a fresh-baked loaf of bread or a main dish of some kind on the doorstep. Members helped with the children during the summer-long visits. Such kindnesses multiplied a hundredfold over the years I remained in that congregation.

In 1984 I remarried. Lyn's three daughters and my three sons made us the Adventist "Brady Bunch." Someone has said that blended families don't really blend; they collide. Our children did their best, but it was a challenge for all of us. Lyn and I love each other deeply, but it has not been easy working through the seemingly endless complications of a second marriage.

I have a closer relationship with Lyn than I've ever had with anyone. But she and I have done something to achieve this that my first wife and I never did—we've sought help. I was too proud to seek aid in my first marriage until it was too late. But Lyn and I have gone for it many times. We've obtained professional help when we needed it, and we've sought the help of friends in the church who have accepted us and let us talk through our problems with them by the hours. One couple, mighty in prayer, literally prayed us through some difficult days. It's made all the difference. We've done it because we care about each other and want to do whatever we can to make our marriage stronger.

Lyn and I schedule our times together as rigidly as we try to schedule our personal times for God. If we don't, we suffer. On occasion we break away for a couple days just to be alone together somewhere. Some of our closest bonding times for me have been the occasions when we read from some devotional book and pray together in an unhurried way. Our goal is to find such time each day. We don't always make it. But we're both realizing that spiritual time together is as important to us as a couple as our private time with God is to each of us individually.

While we haven't arrived at the place we want to be someday, our relationship grows deeper each year. Yet we both know that if we get careless, we could lose the ground we've gained. But we're committed to keep on the journey together. Which is how I understand the way the spiritual relationship works as well.

---

[1] E. G. White, *Selected Messages* (Washington, D.C.: Review and Herald Pub. Assn., 1958, 1980), book 3, p. 217.

[2] Rick Rice, *When Bad Things Happen to God's People* (Boise, Id.: Pacific Press Pub. Assn., 1985), p. 42.

[3] Michele Weiner-Davis, *Divorce Busting: A Revolutionary and Rapid Program for "Staying Together"* (New York: Simon and Schuster, 1992), p. 99.

[4] E. G. White, *Testimonies,* vol. 6, p. 301.

[5] *Ibid.,* vol. 9, p. 189.

LOOKING
WITHIN

PRIDE LUST

selfishness

defeat

CHAPTER NINE

The Ordinary Adventist's Quest to Know God's Will

One of the questions most frequently asked by fellow members who have sought my counsel as a pastor has been, "How can I know what God's will is for me in the particular situation I'm facing?" In addition, it has been such an important concern to me personally that as one of my major devotional projects I once read the Bible through specifically looking for everything I could find related to it.

Scripture prominently reflects the desire to know God's will. Paul admonished the Ephesians: "Do not be foolish, but understand what the Lord's will is" (Eph. 5:17). John wrote, "The world and its desires pass away, but the man who does the will of God lives forever" (1 John 2:17). And Jesus made sure that each time we prayed His prayer, "Your will be done on earth as it is in heaven," we would be seeking for His will to be done in our lives and reminding ourselves of its importance (Matt. 6:10).

How Specific Is God's Will?

David wrote: "My frame was not hidden from you when I was made in the secret place. When I was woven together in the depths of the earth, your eyes saw my unformed body. All the days ordained for me were written in your book before one of them came to be" (Ps. 139:15, 16). *The Living Bible* renders verse 16: "You saw me before I was born and scheduled each day of my life before I began to breathe. Each day was recorded in your Book!" Does God have a book that contains every detail of our lives already planned out for us? Is our search for His will a matter of learning the secret spiritual code that will enable us to detect those details day by day? Ellen White wrote: "Not more surely is the place prepared for us in the heavenly mansions than is the special place designated on earth where we are to work for God."[1] Does God have written in His book what our career should be, whom we should marry, where we should live (state, city, neighborhood) at any given time?

God gave many people in the Bible specific tasks to perform. He told Jeremiah, "Before you were born I set you apart; I appointed you as a prophet to the nations" (Jer. 1:5). When God led Israel out of Egypt, He led them by the hand from place to place by a cloud and pillar of fire (Num. 9:15-23). David routinely asked God whether or not he should go into battle against an enemy, and he received direct answers from God (1 Sam. 23:1-4; 2 Sam. 5:19, 22-25). Once he even asked God what city he should live in, and God answered, "Hebron" (2 Sam. 2:1). Paul received similar directions from God—forbidden at one time by the Holy Spirit to preach in Asia, and at another from entering Bithynia, and once he had a dream that he interpreted as God directing Him to preach in Macedonia (Acts 16:6-10).

However, such divine interventions seemed to be the exception rather than the rule. The miraculous signs God used to direct Paul's missionary itinerary seems to be a deviation from the normal order in which the apostle planned his trips. Normally he based them on prayerful discernment of needs and opportunities, and the counsel of others (Acts 15:36-16:5). When early church leaders needed guidance on specific theological and lifestyle differences that were posing a problem for the unity of the church, they debated the matter frankly and openly, and came to a consensus that "seemed good to the Holy Spirit and to us," as a guide for the growing church (Acts 15:1-35). The office of deacon resulted not by direct command from God, but out of the very practical need for administrative assistants to relieve the apostles of the burden of ministering to the daily necessities of poor people who were becoming Christians (Acts 6:1-7). We could cite many such biblical examples.

From considering all the scriptures I've been able to find on this subject, I've concluded:

1. *In those areas in which God has given direct commandments, His will is specific and is to be obeyed.* This includes the two great commandments of love to God and others, the Ten Commandments, forgiving our enemies, returning good for evil, etc.

2. *In those areas in which God has given no direct commandment, we are both free and responsible to choose the course of action that will bring the greatest honor and glory to God* (1 Cor. 10:31). Many, if not most, of the choices we have to make fall into this category.

An Analogy—Growing Children

I believe that we can find significant parallels between God's will for us and our will for our own children. The younger our children are, the more we make their decisions for them, including their food, clothes, and friends. The older they get and more mature they become, the more we choose to play the role of counselor rather than decision-maker for them. In fact, allowing children to make decisions at graduated levels of responsibility is an indispensable part of the maturation process.

When I was 12, my enthrallment with movies created a Sunday morning ritual at our home. The first thing in the morning I would ask to go to the afternoon matinee at our town theater. The answer was always no. Then came the coaxing and cajoling and persuading for as long as needed until I got to go. It almost always worked. One Sunday I was all prepared for the usual contest, my arguments well in mind. Only this time I was told that I was getting old enough to start making my own decisions about such things. The response left me ecstatic. Now I could go to the matinee every Sunday for the rest of my life! But surprisingly, I kept arguing the issue in my own mind with the Holy Spirit. And before the matinee began that afternoon, I clearly remember deciding that I was not going to ruin my own life on movies. That was the first Sunday in months that I didn't attend. I rarely went again. From that very day the hold that movies had on me was broken.

One of my most gratifying experiences as a parent comes when one of my children seeks my counsel and makes decisions that are clearly their own, but that happen to also reflect my own deeply held values. That's true even though I know my value system isn't yet perfect.

I'm convinced that God's primary will for us focuses on us growing to have such love and respect for Him that we seek His counsel on all decisions of consequence, and then make choices that are truly our own, but that happen to also reflect His values, which *are* perfect. I believe that few things, if any, are more rewarding for God.

What About Signs?

What about the biblical examples of God leading people by direct signs, such as Gideon and his fleece (Judges 6:36-40)? For every such story, we find other scriptures that caution against seeking signs to know God's will. Speaking to His critics who were seeking a sign from Him, Jesus said, "A wicked and adulterous generation asks for a miraculous sign!" (Matt. 12:39). In Jesus' parable of the rich man and Lazarus, when the rich man asked Abraham to send his brothers a sign from the dead, Abraham told him that they had the Scriptures and therefore didn't need a sign (Luke 16:29-31). Concerning certain fanatical displays in early Adventist history, Ellen White said, "In times past certain among the believers had great faith in the setting of signs by which to decide their duty" "[employing] man-made tests for ascertaining a knowledge of the will of God; and I was shown that this was a delusion which became an infatuation, and that it is contrary to the will of the Lord."[2] While God has honored some requests for a sign, it seems not to be His preferred manner of communicating His will.

If knowing God's will is primarily a matter of following divinely sent signs, how do we know for sure when we've picked up the right signals? Two friends immediately come to mind who chose their spouses based on signs they believed God had given them. One of the marriages lasted less than a year, the other has been a troubled marriage right from the start. Concerned friends cautioned both couples against their marriages, but the parties involved chose to "obey God rather than man"!

In some ways it would be much easier if God *would* make all our decisions for us through the revelation of direct signs. It can be scary to feel as though you're the one responsible for a vital choice. No one wants to make a mistake on an important decision. Yet Joseph R. Cooke has expressed the value of even the mistakes we make in this process: "Even our mistakes fit into the pattern. Certain mistakes, in His infinite kindness, He aborts or blocks. Certain others, even very serious ones, He allows to bear their terrible fruit. This turns out to be a kindness. He knows that some of these worst mistakes spring from a radical defect deep down in our hearts, and that the defect will never be corrected unless we see it for what it is through the fruit that it bears. So He lets us fall flat on our faces. He lets us make a mess of things. He lets us lose precious months and even years of our lives. He allows the wounds to pierce deep, deep into our hearts. But when we come through on the other side, we find that God has done something in us and for us that we will be thankful for all our days. Out of folly and ugliness He has brought His own wisdom and beauty." [3]

I've concluded from my study that, as a general rule, the decisions that most honor God and accord with His will are value-based, rather than sign-based. This understanding has led me to desire to know God better, and to seek those principles that lead to choices that honor Him.

Ten Principles
for Making Decisions in Harmony With God's Will

1. Determine That Your Decisions Will Honor God Above All Else

" 'I will instruct thee and teach thee . . . : I will guide thee with mine eye' (Ps. 32:8). . . . If we come to God in a humble and teachable spirit, not with our plans all formed before we ask Him, and shaped according to our own will, but in submission, in willingness to be taught, in faith, it is our privilege to claim the promise every hour of the day. We may distrust ourselves, and we need to guard against our own inclinations and strong tendencies lest we shall follow our mind and plans and think it is the way of the Lord." [4]

George Mueller, one of the outstanding Christian leaders of the past century, described the beginning of his decision-making process in these words: "I seek at the beginning to get my heart into such a state that it has no will of its own in regard to a given matter. . . . Nine tenths of difficulties are overcome when our hearts are ready to do the Lord's will, whatever it may be." [5]

2. Commune With God Through His Word
Through daily communion with God in the study of His Word, for the purpose of getting to know Him better, we expose ourselves to His values, which the Holy Spirit writes on our hearts and in our minds. By this He conditions us to make choices based on divine values (Ps. 119:105).

3. Commune With God in Prayer
Likewise the personal communion with God that comes through prayer likewise prepares us to make decisions based on God's values. James invites us to pray for special wisdom to make choices in accord with His will, and promises that God will give it (James 1:5).

4. Be Attentive to God's Providential Indications
While I believe God prefers decisions that are value-directed rather than sign-directed, the Bible contains an impressive number of exceptions in which God guided decisions more directly. He may use any number of circumstances to provide such direction when He so chooses.

Unless such providences are unmistakably miraculous interventions from God, however, we should not necessarily allow them to overpower a decision that all other factors involved make clear would be better. I accept apparent providences as factors to weigh rather than commands to obey.

5. Do Outside Research When Appropriate
Paul gathered information about the condition of the churches he had raised up so that he might best know how to minister to them (1 Cor. 1:11; 5:1; etc.). When making a decision, get all the facts you can. It's often a good idea to list side by side all of the assets and liabilities of the various options you are considering, and to prayerfully weigh their relative values. This step has been immensely helpful in clarifying a number of difficult decisions for me.

6. Counsel With Godly Counselors
"In an abundance of counselors there is safety" (Prov. 11:14, NRSV). But David warns against "ungodly" counselors (Ps. 1:1). Counseling with others about a matter helps to clarify issues and to

weigh the relative importance of the various factors involved. I find great strength and help in seeking counsel.

After I presented this list to one group, someone handed me this note: "Why is God's will for me different than for my spouse? We both try to follow God's will, and it seems as if God has two wills. When God comes closer, we do not. We both want God in our lives, but seem to chase Him out of each other's lives."

In families in which both spouses seek God's will, it's better to do so together as a couple, rather than merely alone as individuals. I believe God rarely, if ever, leads spouses in ways that will damage their relationship as a couple if they will discuss and pray together sufficiently about the matter. I find that unselfish love and benevolence prompt them to adjust their private view of a matter to be more accommodating to each other, and to be more accepting and respectful of each other's viewpoints. The same principle applies to congregations. The Spirit reveals His will for a local church through wide discussion and much prayer among members.

7. Consider the Lessons Learned From Previous Experience

You may have had related experiences in the past through which God has provided you with lessons and insights that could help you in making a wise decision in the present.

8. View the Decision From a Millennial Perspective

The Adventist understanding of the millennium provides us with a valuable perspective for making decisions. In the millennium I want to be able to look back on my life and feel good about the decisions I'm making today. Once I had to decide whether to sue someone who owed me many thousands of dollars. The attorney told me that it would be one of the easiest cases he'd ever taken, and I was about destitute at the time. But after weighing all the factors, and considering which decision I would rather be able to look back on from the millennial perspective, I decided not to do anything. While I don't think it would have been necessarily unchristian to go to court in this instance, to this day I feel good about the decision that I made. My debtor has become a friend, and I believe my decision could yet be an influence for eternal life.

9. After Prayerfully Weighing All the Factors, Make a Decision

Ellen White encourages us to "consult sanctified reason" before making a decision.[6] How do you know that you're making the best possible decision? You don't. But as Joseph R. Cooke encourages:

"God does not hold us responsible for making the one and only perfect decision at every turn of life's road. He asks us only to do the best we can. In the learning process we are bound to make many, many mistakes. But these need not be cause for dismay or discouragement, for, as we continue to take the responsibility of using to the full our modicum of spiritual wisdom, we grow in our ability to choose and to do those things that most please our Lord."[7]

If you're going through a severe crisis and find yourself mentally and emotionally incapable of making the decisions required of you, you might rely on the counsel of someone whose judgment you trust the most. During such a crisis in my life, I took verbatim the counsel of a trusted friend. Not everything turned out perfectly, but the results were no doubt better than if I had made my decisions on my own in the troubled state of mind I was in at the time.

At times you would be justified in refraining from making a decision until you could regain your equilibrium. "Often your mind may be clouded because of pain. Then do not try to think. You know that Jesus loves you. He understands your weakness. You may do His will by simply resting in His arms."[8]

10. Ask for a Settled Peace About the Decision

George Mueller said, "Through prayer to God, the study of the Word, and reflection, I come to a deliberate judgment according to the best of my ability and knowledge; and if my mind is thus at peace, and continues so after two or three more petitions, I proceed accordingly."[9] I ask God to give me that peace if the decision I'm making is honorable to Him.

Submit All Decisions and Plans to God

James admonished: "Listen, you who say, 'Today or tomorrow we will go to this or that city, spend a year there, carry on business and make money.' Why, you do not even know what will happen tomorrow. . . . Instead, you ought to say, 'If it is the Lord's will, we will live and do this or that'" (James 4:13-15). Paul told the

Christians at Rome, "I planned many times to come to you (but have been prevented from doing so until now)" (Rom. 1:13). Paul trusted the all-seeing wisdom of God to intervene and change his plans as God deemed appropriate. On this theme Ellen White wrote:

"Lay all your plans before God, to be carried out or given up, as His providence shall indicate. Accept His plans instead of your own, even though their acceptance requires the abandonment of cherished projects."[10]

The weight of biblical evidence suggests to me that God intervenes only sparingly to override the choices of His children who are doing their best to make value-based decisions that honor Him. If He does, it will be unmistakably clear.

Jesus and the Will of God

Did Jesus make plans for His life? *The Desire of Ages* says: "The Son of God was surrendered to the Father's will, and dependent upon His power. So utterly was Christ emptied of self that He made no plans for Himself. He accepted God's plans for Him and day by day the Father unfolded His plans. So should we depend upon God, that our lives may be the simple outworking of His will."[11]

I once worked with a man who tried to live like this. It was a frustrating experience for me. He not only resisted my efforts to make plans for the church, but he felt it was a sin for me even to prepare a shopping list before I went to the store!

Then I found other statements from the same author that went like this: "The great Teacher laid plans for His work. Study these plans."[12] "It is essential to labor with order, following an organized plan and a definite object."[13] "We are altogether too narrow in our plans. We need to be broader minded. . . . We must get away from our smallness and make larger plans."[14]

When I studied Jesus' life, it resolved this apparent contradiction. The lesson I learned was awesome.

Jesus devoted Himself entirely to knowing and doing God's desire for Him. "My food," Jesus said, "is to do the will of him who sent me and to finish his work" (John 4:34). "By myself I can do nothing; . . . I seek not to please myself but him who sent me" (John 5:30). "I have come down from heaven not to do my will but to do the will of him who sent me" (John 6:38). "I have brought you glory on earth by completing the work you gave me to do" (John

17:4). How could Jesus have come to know God's will so thoroughly that His life could be said to be "the simple outworking of His will"?

The key, I believe, appears in Isaiah 50:4, 5, which prophesies of the Lord's Messianic Servant: "The Sovereign Lord has given me an instructed tongue, to know the word that sustains the weary. He wakens me morning by morning, wakens my ear to listen like one being taught. The Sovereign Lord has opened my ears, and I have not been rebellious; I have not drawn back."

Even a casual reading of the Gospels reveals how Scripture saturated His mind. Not only did He overcome temptation with Scripture (Matt. 4:1-11), but His teachings were laced with it (Matt. 5-7). He met His accusers with Scripture (Matt. 12:1-8), ministered with Scripture (John 7:37, 38), and gave warnings with Scripture (Matt. 24:36-39). He had hid His Father's Word in His heart that He might not sin against Him (Ps. 119:11). God's Word was the joy and rejoicing of His heart (see Jer. 15:16).

"From hours spent with God He came forth morning by morning to bring the light of heaven to men. Daily He received a fresh baptism of the Holy Spirit. In the early hours of the new day the Lord awakened Him from His slumbers, and His soul and His lips were anointed with grace, that He might impart to others. His words were given Him fresh from the heavenly courts, words that He might speak in season to the weary and oppressed." [15]

Jesus didn't need a list of 10 principles on how to make choices in harmony with God's will. To Him there was but one all-absorbing principle. He began the day in communion with His Father. During those early-morning hours He became imbued with the Father's values and dreams and goals and character traits. He came forth from those hours of communion with His agenda, His plans, for the day to share His Father's love in specific ways. But even though He crafted His daily to-do list during moments of communion with God, Jesus still submitted His plans to His Father, to be carried out or given up as the Father's providence would indicate. The specifics of His agenda could change at any time, because He remained in communion with God throughout the day, and He was thoroughly sensitive to the people and the events and the needs around Him, and responded in whatever way He believed would bring the greatest glory to God.

Jesus didn't need to put out fleeces to know God's will. He saw God's providences manifested in the people who surrounded Him day by day, in their openness or resistance to His invitations, in their reactions and responses to His word. Gadarenes was one of the privileged towns of earth to get a visit from Him, but they asked Him to leave only hours after His arrival (Luke 8:26-37). So He left, for it's one of His Father's values never to force Himself on anyone. But when the town of Samaria asked Him to stay with them for several days instead of merely passing through as He had planned, He adjusted His itinerary to meet their awakened spiritual hunger (John 4:40). Or when He passed under the sycamore tree on His way out of town, and spotted the little man in the expensive robe perched on a branch overhead, He altered His plans for lunch to take advantage of this unusual expression of interest (Luke 19:1-10). He was alive every moment to His surroundings, in dynamic interaction with His environment, seizing every opportunity of speaking a word of consolation to the weary or warning to the careless, wherever and whenever He discerned it might be welcomed or needed. Just like His Father, He did unto others what He would have wanted done to Himself were He in their place. To do so, He knew, was always His Father's will.

To every ordinary Adventist the very same invitation and offer arrives at the beginning of every day, just as it came to Jesus. "The Sovereign Lord has given me an instructed tongue, to know the word that sustains the weary. He wakens me morning by morning, wakens my ear to listen like one being taught. The Sovereign Lord has opened my ears, and I have not been rebellious; I have not drawn back" (Isa. 50:4, 5). His testimony can be ours, if we will make it so.

"And if we [thus] consent, He will so identify Himself with our thoughts and aims, so blend our hearts and minds into conformity to His will, that when obeying Him we shall be but carrying out our own impulses."[16]

---

[1] E. G. White, *Christ's Object Lessons,* p. 327.

[2] ———— , *Selected Messages,* book 2, p. 28.

[3] Joseph R. Booke, *Celebration of Grace* (Grand Rapids: Zondervan, 1991), p. 118.

[4] E. G. White, *Our Father Cares,* p. 134.

[5] S. Maxwell Coder, *God's Will for Your Life* (Chicago: Moody Press, 1946), p. 80.

[6] E. G. White, *Medical Ministry* (Mountain View, Calif.: Pacific Press Pub. Assn., 1932), p. 99.

[7] Cooke, p. 115.
[8] E. G. White, *The Ministry of Healing,* p. 251.
[9] In Coder, p. 80.
[10] E. G. White, *Testimonies,* vol. 7, p. 44.
[11] ———— , *The Desire of Ages,* p. 208.
[12] ———— , *Evangelism* (Washington, D.C.: Review and Herald Pub. Assn., 1946), p. 53.
[13] *Ibid.,* p. 94.
[14] *Ibid.,* p. 46.
[15] ———— , *Christ's Object Lessons,* p. 139.
[16] ———— , *The Desire of Ages,* p. 668.

CHAPTER TEN

The Ordinary
Adventist's Fear
of the Final Crisis

Gary Burns, a former youth pastor at the Pioneer Memorial church at Andrews University, reported to our staff one day that all the youth groups from seventh grade and up that he has worked with over the years, when asked to identify their major concerns, have always included the same two issues at the top of their lists: How to know if they are ready for Jesus to return, and fear over whether or not they will be able to stand through the time of trouble they've heard is coming. The only close runners-up are concerns relating to specific lifestyle issues they may be struggling with.

Can you identify with these fears about the great time of trouble the Bible predicts will occur before Jesus returns? When you hear new evidences that the end of the world may be near, do you sense any anxiety about your own readiness for it? If the prophesied crisis were to break over the world next week, would you feel prepared to go through it victoriously?

For some of us, such questions may seem closer to the twilight zone than to real life. Our schedules are so jammed full these days, who has time to worry about future events that may never happen during our lifetimes anyway? Talk of a time of trouble, a final crisis, may seem more like a surrealistic illusion than an impending reality. Real life looks more like going to work, shopping, building or remodeling, watching a sitcom, working on a relationship or recovering from one, keeping caught up on the news, saving for a vacation, wondering why the Visa bill is so high this month, and trying to juggle scores of competing demands on our time each day.

Jesus said the final generation would be like this, just like that generation long ago who continued "eating and drinking, marrying and giving in marriage, . . . and they knew nothing about what would happen until the flood came and took them all away. That is how it will be at the coming of the Son of Man" (Matt. 24:38, 39).

An Ominous Warning

During one of the commercials between Willard Scott's weather report and the interview with Dolly Parton on the next *Today* show, try dubbing in this 60-second sound bite:

"A third angel followed them and said in a loud voice: 'If anyone worships the beast and his image and receives his mark on the forehead or on the hand, he, too, will drink of the wine of God's fury, which has been poured full strength into the cup of his wrath. He will be tormented with burning sulfur in the presence of the holy angels and of the Lamb. And the smoke of their torment rises for ever and ever. There is no rest day or night for those who worship the beast and his image, or for anyone who receives the mark of his name'" (Rev. 14:9-11).

The Bible identifies this third angel's message as the last message to go to the world prior to the return of Jesus. It appears that God has resorted to shock-effect language in an attempt to startle our generation awake from its perilous computer-crazed, sports-crazed, academia-crazed, professionalism-crazed, accomplishment-crazed, information-crazed, addiction-crazed stupor. Perhaps gentler language would not have gotten our attention. He took a great risk using such language, which many have interpreted as indicating a threatening, vengeful God. In reality, it's the language of a loving Parent who's shouting a desperate warning to His children who have strayed into the path of a killer storm—the second death of all who withdraw themselves irrevocably from the life-sustaining presence of God. But before that storm hits, the Bible says we will encounter a time of trouble the likes of which the world has not yet seen.

The Crisis Ahead—Worst Ever!

"At that time Michael, the great prince, the protector of your people, shall arise. There shall be a time of anguish, such as has never occurred since nations first came into existence" (Dan. 12:1, NRSV). Jesus reiterated this warning: "Then there will be great distress, unequaled from the beginning of the world until now—and never to be equaled again. If those days had not been cut short, no one would survive, but for the sake of the elect those days will be shortened" (Matt. 24:21, 22). As Revelation 13 describes this final crisis, the entire world community will try to kill all those who refuse to worship the beast or receive its mark in their forehead or hand (Rev. 13:15-17).

While He endured the excruciating torture His persecutors subjected Him to before they crucified Him, Jesus looked down to the end of time and lamented, "If men do these things when the tree is green, what will happen when it is dry?" (Luke 23:31). It is yet to be seen what hideous acts of cruelty will strike God's people once human beings turn their backs irrevocably on God, and mercy no longer tempers their actions.

Commenting on these warnings, Ellen White wrote: "The 'time of trouble, such as never was,' is soon to open upon us; and we shall need an experience which we do not now possess, and which many are too indolent to obtain. It is often the case that trouble is greater in anticipation than in reality; but this is not true of the crisis before us. The most vivid presentation cannot reach the magnitude of the ordeal."[1] "Many will be imprisoned, many will flee for their lives from cities and towns, and many will be martyrs for Christ's sake in standing in defense of the truth."[2]

At the very time that I am rooting for the Chicago Bulls to win another world championship, an ominous reality looms large on history's horizon.

Naturally I don't like to think much about this. After all, I have a hard enough time going to the dentist, let alone being threatened with persecution. The thought of being tortured for my faith frightens me. I've read stories of the prison camps during the Holocaust that I can't get out of my mind, the horrible things done there to people. Lyn and I recently read Noble Alexander's story, *I Will Die Free.* Imprisoned and tortured for his faith for more than 20 years in Castro's infamous prison system before Jesse Jackson was finally able to negotiate his release, he refused to deny his faith even once during that time. Every time we would read a new chapter of his story, about new forms of torture he endured, I would turn to Lyn and confess, "I don't think I could survive that one."

And yet my greatest concern in all of this is not so much the physical pain, as frightening as that is for me to think about. I'm even more concerned that under pressure I might deny Christ as Peter did on the night of His betrayal. Under persecution, would I be among those who "did not love their lives so much as to shrink from death" (Rev. 12:11)? What if my persecutors were to bring one of my children before me, threatening to persecute my child unless I deny my faith in Christ? What would I do?

I've watched interviews of several POWs returned from Vietnam. They described the forms of torture the Viet Cong inflicted upon them, and how they eventually broke down and volunteered information that may have aided the enemy. These were not weak men, but they were pushed beyond the limits of their endurance. What would I do if so tested for my faith?

I don't believe God wants us to become preoccupied with such questions, but His awesome warnings of what is coming must constantly remind us that life is not one big party from which we never have to go home. The awareness that we may be the generation to experience the unparalleled time of trouble that's been prophesied for millennia should inspire us to a spiritual watchfulness and earnestness every day of our lives. "Be careful," Jesus warned, "or your hearts will be weighed down with dissipation, drunkenness and the anxieties of life, and that day will close on you unexpectedly like a trap. For it will come upon all those who live on the face of the whole earth. Be always on the watch, and pray that you may be able to escape all that is about to happen, and that you may be able to stand before the Son" (Luke 21:34-36).

How to Prepare for the Final Crisis

1. Trust God to Make the Needed Provision

As I discussed in chapter 4, I believe that it's a mistake to interpret the oft-quoted promise of Psalm 91: "No evil shall befall you, no scourge come near your tent" (verse 10, NRSV) to mean that God's people will not suffer when the crisis comes. Just too many texts warn of intense suffering during that time. But I believe that the true meaning of that promise is even better news than protection from physical suffering—God will make whatever provision needed to keep the faith of His trusting children from breaking in the hour of severe trial. I believe this is the meaning of Psalm 34:19: "Many are the afflictions of the righteous, but the Lord rescues them from them all" (NRSV). It must also be what Jesus had in mind when He both warned and assured His disciples in the same breath: "You will be delivered up even by parents and brothers and kinsmen and friends, and some of you they will put to death [in the physical sense]; . . . But not a hair of your head will perish [in the spiritual sense, because their faith would be strengthened, enabling them to endure to the end]" (Luke 21:16-18, RSV).

Corrie ten Boom tells a story that illustrates this point. Corrie grew up in Haarlem, Holland, and lived in the Beje (their house) with her family (including sisters Betsie and Nollie, and aunt "Tante" Jans) during the early days of World War II, before their deportation to the concentration camp in which all her family but herself perished. Each Monday Corrie rode the train to Amsterdam with her father, a watchmaker, so he could set his watch accurately at the Naval Observatory. One day Corrie accompanied her mother and sister Nollie to visit Mrs. Hoog, a neighbor whose baby had just died. I'll let Corrie tell the story from here.

"Mama went at once to the young mother, but I stood frozen on the threshold. Just to the right of the door, so still in the homemade crib, was the baby. . . .

"I stood staring at the tiny unmoving form with my heart thudding strangely against my ribs. Nollie, always braver than I, stretched out her hand and touched the ivory-white cheek. I longed to do it too, but hung back, afraid. For a while curiosity and terror struggled in me. At last I put one finger on the small curled hand.

"It was cold.

"Cold as we walked back to the Beje, cold as I washed for supper, cold even in the snug gas-lit dining room. Between me and each familiar face around the table crept those small icy fingers. For all Tante Jans's talk about it, death had been only a word. Now I knew that it could really happen—if to the baby, then to Mama, to Father, to Betsie!

"Still shivering with that cold, I followed Nollie up to our room and crept into bed beside her. At last we heard Father's footsteps winding up the stairs. It was the best moment in every day, when he came up to tuck us in. We never fell asleep until he had arranged the blankets in his special way and laid his hand for a moment on each head. Then we tried not to move even a toe.

"But that night as he stepped through the door I burst into tears. 'I need you!' I sobbed. 'You can't die! You can't!'

"Beside me on the bed Nollie sat up. 'We went to see Mrs. Hoog,' she explained. 'Corrie didn't eat her supper or anything.'

"Father sat down on the edge of the narrow bed. 'Corrie,' he began gently, 'when you and I go to Amsterdam—when do I give you your ticket?'

"I sniffed a few times, considering this.

" 'Why, just before we get on the train.'

" 'Exactly. And our wise Father in heaven knows when we're going to need things, too. Don't run out ahead of Him, Corrie. When the time comes that some of us will have to die, you will look into your heart and find the strength you need—just in time.' "[3]

Ellen White concurs: "The disciples were not endowed with the courage and fortitude of the martyrs until such grace was needed."[4] Paul testified similarly: "I know whom I have believed, and am convinced that he is able to guard what I have entrusted to him for that day" (2 Tim. 1:12). In his benedictory doxology, Jude glorified God "who is able to keep you from falling and to present you before his glorious presence without fault and with great joy" (Jude 24).

2. Seize the Spiritual Opportunities Each Day Brings

Jesus admonished, "Be always on the watch, and pray that you may be able to escape all that is about to happen, and that you may be able to stand before the Son" (Luke 21:36, KJV). I'm convinced that *the best way for me to prepare for the final crisis is by being faithful to the spiritual opportunities and challenges that I am confronted with today.* Marvin Moore concludes similarly in his excellent book *The Crisis of the End Time:*

"The most important question this book addresses: How can you and I keep our relationship with Jesus in earth's darkest hour? And here's my answer: You and I must have a relationship with Jesus *before* we enter earth's darkest hour if we expect to have it *in* earth's darkest hour." "If you are not developing a close relationship with Jesus now, you may receive the mark of the beast even while professing to believe the Sabbath." "I simply cannot stress enough that you and I must be developing a spiritual experience now that will enable us to be loyal then."[5]

Prepare for the Big One by Preparing for Today

Ellen White says, "The only way in which men will be able to stand firm in the conflict is to be rooted and grounded in Christ. They must receive the truth as it is in Jesus."[6] Seeking Jesus today is the answer to our preparation for the crisis tomorrow.

Jesus instructed, "Do not worry about tomorrow, for tomorrow will worry about itself. Each day has enough trouble of its own" (Matt. 6:34). *God will allow the very tests and trials to come to us day by day that are calculated to prepare us for the final crisis.* As we take seriously the temptations and trials that afflict us today, meeting their spiritual challenges and gaining from their spiritual opportunities, we are making the needed preparation for the big one at the end.

"Consecrate yourself to God in the morning; make this your very first work. Let your prayer be, 'Take me, O Lord, as wholly Thine. I lay all my plans at Thy feet. Use me today in Thy service. Abide with me, and let all my work be wrought in Thee.' This is a daily matter. Each morning consecrate yourself to God for that day."[7]

"This is a daily matter." That's how the preparation for the final crisis takes place—one day at a time. We seek God in the quiet place, one day at a time. He seals us with His seal, one day at a time. The latter rain of the Holy Spirit moistens us, one day at a time. The mark of the beast is likewise received, one day at a time. If we are faithful to God today, "tomorrow will worry about itself."

"Christ has given us no promise of help in bearing today the burdens of tomorrow. He has said, 'My grace is sufficient for thee' (2 Cor. 12:9); but, like the manna given in the wilderness, His grace is bestowed daily, for the day's need. Like the hosts of Israel in their pilgrim life, we may find morning by morning the bread of heaven for the day's supply.

"One day alone is ours, and during this day we are to live for God. For this one day we are to place in the hand of Christ, in solemn service, all our purposes and plans, casting all our care upon Him, for He careth for us."[8]

One of Lyn's gifts to me that I cherish is a poster that bears this inscription:

"I was regretting the past and fearing the future. Suddenly my Lord was speaking:

"'My name is I AM.'

"He paused. I waited. He continued.

"'When you live in the past, with its mistakes and regrets, it is hard. I am not there. My name is not I Was.

"'When you live in the future with its problems and fears, it is hard. I am not there. My name is not I Will Be.

"'When you live in this moment, it is not hard. I am here. My name is I AM.'"

3. Tune In to Jesus' Voice

Jesus said the final deceptions would be so great that "if it were possible, they shall deceive the very elect" (Matt. 24:24, KJV). I like to think that I am smart enough to see through the David Koreshes of the world. But I can imagine some scenarios of deception that would be very hard for me to distinguish the true from the false. When the great imposter comes with his masterful deceptions, what will keep us from being deceived?

Jesus answered that question when He described the relationship between Himself, "the good Shepherd," and His people, His "sheep," in these words: "The sheep listen to his voice. He calls his own sheep by name and leads them out. . . . His sheep follow him because they know his voice. But they will never follow a stranger; in fact, they will run away from him because they do not recognize a stranger's voice" (John 10:3-5).

Are you tuning in to the voice of Jesus at the beginning of every day? Are you learning to recognize that voice as you seek Him daily in the quiet place? Or is the first voice you hear the voice of your favorite morning newscaster? Do you spend more time listening to Donahue's voice, or Oprah's, or Rush's, than you do to the voice of Jesus? It's a spiritual law that any voice you listen to long enough will begin to sound like the voice of a safe shepherd. The only way to recognize His voice and stay tuned to it when the great deception and final crisis comes is to be listening to His voice in the private hour of prayer and Bible study today.

4. Cultivate the Discipline of Simplicity

Jesus warned against becoming weighed down with "the anxieties of life," lest the final crisis "close on you unexpectedly like a trap" (Luke 21:34). Instead He instructed us to seek first the kingdom of God (Matt. 6:33). I believe Richard Foster rightly interprets Jesus' words as a call to greater simplicity of life:

"Freedom from anxiety is one of the inward evidences of seeking the kingdom of God first. The inward reality of simplicity involves a life of joyful unconcern for possessions. Neither the greedy nor the miserly know that liberty. It has nothing to do with abundance of possessions or their lack. It is an inward spirit of trust. The sheer fact that a person is living without things is no guarantee that he or she is living in simplicity. Paul taught us that the love of money is the root of all evil, and often those who have it the least, love it the most. . . . Conversely, wealth does not bring freedom from anxiety. . . .

"Freedom from anxiety is characterized by three inner attitudes. . . .

"To receive what we have as a gift from God is the first inner attitude of simplicity. . . . When we are tempted to think that what we own is the result of our personal efforts, it takes only a little drought or a small accident to show us once again how radically dependent we are for everything.

"To know that it is God's business, and not ours, to care for what we have is the second inner attitude of simplicity. God is able to protect what we possess. We can trust Him. Does that mean that we should never take the keys out of the car or lock the door? Of course not. But we know that the lock on the door is not what protects the house. It is only common sense to observe normal precaution, but if we believe that it is precaution that protects us and our goods we will be riddled with anxiety. . . . Obviously these matters are not restricted to possessions but include such things as our reputation or our employment. Simplicity means the freedom to trust God for these (and all) things.

"To have our goods available to others marks the third inner attitude of simplicity. Martin Luther said somewhere, 'If our goods are not available to the community, they are stolen goods.' The reason we find these words so difficult is our fear of the future. We cling to our possessions rather than sharing them because we are anxious about tomorrow. But if we truly believe that God is who Jesus said He is, then . . . we can share because we know that He will care for us. If someone is in need we are free to help them. Again, ordinary common sense will define the parameters of our sharing and save us from foolishness.

"When we are seeking first the kingdom of God these three attitudes will characterize our lives."[9]

5. Follow All That Jesus Teaches

Jesus ended His sermon on the mount with a story about a great storm. As all good Sabbath school children know, the house built upon the rock by a wise man withstood the storm. But it destroyed the house erected by a foolish man upon the sand. I believe it's legitimate to understand the storm in Jesus' story to represent the final crisis, and the houses to represent the kinds of people who will stand or fall when the crisis hits. Jesus said the wise man, whose house withstood the storm, represents "everyone who hears these words of mine and puts them into practice," and the foolish man, whose house crashed, represents "everyone who hears these words of mine and does not put them into practice" (Matt. 7:24-26).

And there's the rub, isn't it? Daily putting into practice everything we know we should be doing. The agonizing struggle to accomplish that is the subject of our next chapter.

-----

[1] E. G. White, *The Great Controversy* (Mountain View, Calif.: Pacific Press Pub. Assn., 1911), p. 622.

[2] ———— , *Selected Messages,* book 3, p. 397.

[3] Corrie ten Boom, *The Hiding Place* (Old Tappan, N.J.: Fleming H. Revell, 1971), pp. 28, 29.

[4] E. G. White, *The Desire of Ages,* p. 354.

[5] Marvin Moore, *The Crisis of the End Time* (Boise, Idaho: Pacific Press Pub. Assn., 1992), pp. 43, 133, 145.

[6] E. G. White, *Last Day Events* (Boise, Idaho: Pacific Press Pub. Assn., 1992), p. 151.

[7] ———— , *Steps to Christ,* p. 70.

[8] ———— , *Thoughts From the Mount of Blessing,* p. 101.

[9] R. T. Foster, *Celebration of Discipline,* pp. 77, 78.

CHAPTER ELEVEN

The Ordinary Adventist's Quiet Agony

I've heard many devout Adventist Christians testify of their continual struggle against sin over which they feel that they never seem to gain the complete victory. For one who wants to be completely faithful to God in every respect, such an enduring struggle can be agonizing. We don't often talk to each other about our specific vulnerabilities to sin because we're eager to put our best foot forward in public. And who wants to be constantly speaking of failure all the time when it could have a negative influence on others? Hence, our spiritual struggles against sin often occur in silence, and the agony we feel in the fray of the struggle is a quiet agony. This sometimes results in intense feelings of spiritual loneliness and isolation.

Scripture speaks of the "struggle against sin" as a continual reality encountered by every true child of God (Heb. 12:4). The Christian life is by definition a spiritual warfare: "Our struggle is not against flesh and blood, but against the rulers, against the authorities, against the powers of this dark world and against the spiritual forces of evil in the heavenly realms" (Eph. 6:12). This is more than a reference to spiritual warfare as a generalized theological concept. In candid self-disclosure, Paul wrote of his own personal experience as one who felt the pull of sin deep in his own heart every day.

"I do not understand what I do. For what I want to do I do not do, but what I hate I do. . . . I have the desire to do what is good, but I cannot carry it out. For what I do is not the good I want to do; no, the evil I do not want to do—this I keep on doing. . . . When I want to do good, evil is right there with me. For in my inner being I delight in God's law; but I see another law at work in the members of my body, waging war against the law of my mind and making me a prisoner of the law of sin at work within my members. What a wretched man I am! Who will rescue me from this body of death?" (Rom. 7:15-24). His confession affirms the spiritual agony of all of us who quietly fight our private battles with temptation and sin.

You may be aware that some theologians claim that the passage applies to Paul's preconversion experience only. But regardless of how one interprets Romans 7:15-24 theologically, I can testify that its language depicts what often goes on inside my own mind. I have a terrible struggle with sin. I suppose it would be unfair of me to say that everyone should have to feel the intensity of the war against sin to the same extent that I do—I should be thankful for those who find it easier. But I do know that I am not completely alone. Paul felt it too. And so do many other ordinary Adventists who have confided in me. If you feel the intensity of the battle against sin in your life, I hope you feel better just being assured that you're normal. You're definitely an ordinary Adventist.

A Warfare as Long as Life Shall Last

As I grew up in the church, it never occurred to me that my ministers might have to struggle with pride, selfishness, intemperance, lust, or watching too much football. As they preached to us each Sabbath, it seemed to me that the Christian life came naturally for them. But having been a minister myself now for 25 years, I find that some Christian ideals don't come natural for me even yet. I still act so selfishly at times that it makes me wonder if I was ever truly converted. And I wish that I could say that my failures were limited to selfishness alone. Sometimes I'll be sitting at my desk, or driving down the road, or even sitting on the platform at church, and I'll get the most horribly sinful thoughts. Or I'll walk away from the table so overfull and drowsy that I know it'll be several hours before I can think clearly again. Or I'll neglect to return an important phone call in order to watch some mindless situation comedy.

Paul, speaking expressly of his inner spiritual life as a minister, said, "I keep under my body, and bring it into subjection: lest that by any means, when I have preached to others, I myself should be a castaway" (1 Cor. 9:27, KJV). It doesn't sound to me as though it came particularly easy for him, either.

Commenting on the apostle's self-disclosure, Ellen White wrote: "Paul knew that his warfare against evil would not end so long as life should last. . . . With all his power he continued to strive against natural inclinations. . . . His words, his practices, his passions—all were brought under the control of the Spirit of God. . . .

"He knew that in order to reach Christ's ideal for them (the Corinthian believers), they had before them a life struggle from which there would be no release."[1]

The particulars of the spiritual struggle may change along the way. I stole a candy bar from a store when I was a young boy, and after a Week of Prayer at school I had to go back to the store manager and make it right. Today, however, I'm more likely to succumb to professional jealousy, or to think that I am better than one of my parishioners, or to neglect some known duty I feel God has called me to. But it's essentially the same struggle honed to a more sophisticated level.

The Agony of Defeat

Perhaps the spiritual warfare wouldn't be so agonizing if I were experiencing an uninterrupted series of victories. I know that's not completely true because Jesus, who successfully resisted every temptation, suffered infinitely greater from the warfare than I have, as Scripture reminds me: "In your struggle against sin, you have not yet resisted to the point of shedding your blood" (Heb. 12:4). Nevertheless, the number of setbacks I experience in my struggle against sin is part of my quiet agony. Ellen White explains why every apparent setback, however, may not necessarily mean that one is losing ground in the Christian walk: "The closer you come to Jesus, the more faulty you will appear in your own eyes; for your vision will be clearer, and your imperfections will be seen in broad and distinct contrast to His perfect nature. This is evidence that Satan's delusions have lost their power; that the vivifying influence of the Spirit of God is arousing you."[2]

In other words, I may have more cause for alarm if I *do not* feel the intensity of the spiritual warfare than if I *do*. "No deep-seated love for Jesus can dwell in the heart that does not realize its own sinfulness. . . . If we do not see our own moral deformity, it is un-mistakable evidence that we have not had a view of the beauty and excellence of Christ."[3]

This should not make us neurotic spiritual navel-gazers, but it should be a warning to prevent us from settling into a comfortable religious experience that fails to strive toward the full accomplishment of God's purpose for us—that we be "conformed to the likeness of his Son" (Rom. 8:29).

David dared to pray: "Search me, O God, and know my heart; test me and know my anxious thoughts. See if there is any offensive way in me, and lead me in the way everlasting" (Ps. 139:23, 24). That's a remarkable prayer. The psalmist and king really must have wanted to have his life purified of sin so that he could bear God's image in his life. I doubt that he would have prayed such a prayer unless he knew that God had no desire to shame or condemn him. He must have recognized that God is eager to help turn our weaknesses into strengths when we invite Him to.

My Difficulties With This Second Half

Thus far this chapter has been relatively easy for me to write. Not so for the last half. For I must now discuss what it takes to achieve victory over sin. Not that I don't think what I'm about to share is important. But two things bother me at this point. The first is that discussions of this type often leave the impression that the Christian life is a kind of spiritual shooting gallery in which the main object is to keep knocking down sins as they pop up endlessly before you. That connotation repulses me. True Christianity is nothing of the sort. It is daily living in relationship with God in a way that infuses the whole of life with joy and meaning and purpose.

But then too, Christianity is spiritual warfare that taxes us to the utmost and leaves us bone-weary at times. We have been assured that Christ has won the decisive battle and even the war itself, and that our personal battles with sin are merely part of the mopping-up maneuvers. But we also know that the enemy can still inflict heavy casualties on those who fail to watch and pray lest they succumb to temptation.

The second reason I've had a hard time writing about how to achieve victory over sin is even more formidable. As I've already confessed, I'm not always victorious over sin myself. And a little voice keeps reminding me of this and asking me what right I have to talk to others about how to achieve victory over sin. Very sensitive to the charge Physician, heal thyself, I'm keenly aware that this physician still has a long way to go. What enables me to continue with this chapter are examples such as the apostle Paul who toward the end of his life still felt himself to be the worst of sinners (1 Tim. 1:15).

With these caveats clearly in mind, I will now share several important steps I've discovered that have enabled me to gain the ground I have thus far in the spiritual warfare.

Steps to Victory

1. Recognize Your Dependence Upon God for Spiritual Victories

Because "our struggle is not against flesh and blood, but against . . . the spiritual forces of evil in the heavenly realms," we must have the direct intervention of God or we will lose many battles and eventually become a casualty of the war (Eph. 6:12). Jesus said, "Apart from me you can do nothing" (John 15:5). This reality should make us fearful of engaging the battle for a single day without taking time to link up with Jesus.

Lyn made a tole painting of one of my favorite texts, Exodus 14:14: "The Lord will fight for you; you need only to be still." Hung over my desk, it reminds me of Israel's helplessness when the Egyptians were about to push them into the Red Sea. Moses assured them with the words of Exodus 14:14. God asked them to do something, to start marching toward the sea. It wasn't much. But when they did it, He did the rest. I find this principle all through Scripture. It has to be woven all through our lives.

Hebrews 4:16 invites, "Let us therefore approach the throne of grace with boldness, so that we may receive mercy and find grace to help in time of need" (NRSV). Morris Venden helped me to understand that this text does not advocate waiting until the temptation comes before seeking help from God. He suggests its meaning to be Let us approach the throne of grace now, at the beginning of each day in study and prayer, so that we may receive mercy and find grace to help later, when the temptations come. Dependence upon God for strength to meet temptation is more than an emergency measure—it's a lifestyle.

2. Ask God for the Ability to Recognize Sin and Resist It While It's Still in the Temptation Stage

"Each one is tempted when, by his own evil desire, he is dragged away and enticed. Then, after desire has conceived, it gives birth to sin; and sin, when it is full-grown, gives birth to death" (James 1:14, 15). According to James, Satan aims his temptations at our minds and desires. Marvin Moore suggests a key step in victory over sin is praying for God to take away the desire for a specific sin:

"For myself, I do not know of any spiritual battle that is more difficult than asking God to change my desire for a particular sin when I want nothing more right then than to do it. However, I have found that when I say that prayer at my moment of strongest temptation, I gain the victory. I've also found that if I keep asking Him to change my desire each time that temptation presents itself to me, eventually I come to the place that I no longer want that sin."[4]

I have found Moore's strategy to be helpful for my own spiritual battles. However, I don't do as well if I wait for the temptation to come before I ask God to remove the desire for a particular sin. In my specific vulnerabilities where I know a sin is deep-rooted in my life, I pray for God to do whatever it takes to root out any vestiges of desire for it. That is not an easy prayer for me to pray because I know that when it's answered, the behavior in question will no longer be as attractive to me or have the same "reward" for me as it's had in the past. This forces me to confront my love for sin.

Neil T. Anderson finds three texts to hold the key to nipping temptation in the bud, beginning with 1 Corinthians 10:13:

"'No temptation has overtaken you but such as is common to man; and God is faithful, who will not allow you to be tempted beyond what you are able, but with the temptation will provide the way of escape also, that you may be able to endure it' (NASB). Where is the escape hatch that Paul is talking about here? In the same place temptation introduces itself: in your mind. Every temptation is first a thought begun in your mind by your own carnality or the tempter himself. If you ruminate on that thought and consider it an option, you will eventually act on it, and that's sin. Instead Paul instructs us to take every thought captive to the obedience of Christ (2 Cor. 10:5). The first step for escaping temptation is to apprehend every thought as soon as it steps through the doorway of your mind.

"Once you have halted a penetrating thought, the next step is to evaluate it on the basis of Paul's eightfold criterion for what we should think about: 'Whatever is true, whatever is honorable, whatever is right, whatever is pure, whatever is lovely, whatever is of good repute, if there is any excellence and if anything worthy of praise, let your mind dwell on these things' (Phil. 4:8, NASB). Ask yourself, 'Does this thought line up with God's truth? Is it suggesting that I do something honorable? Right? Pure? If this thought becomes action, will the outcome be lovely and contribute to excellence in my life? Will other believers approve of my actions? Is it something for which I can praise God?' If the answer to any of those questions is no, dismiss that thought immediately. Don't have anything more to do with it. If it keeps coming back, keep saying no. When you learn to respond to tempting thoughts by stopping them at the door of your mind, evaluating them on the basis of God's Word, and dismissing those that fail the test, you have found the way of escape that God's Word promises."[5]

3. Whenever a Temptation Crosses Over the Line to Become Sin and You Become Aware of It, Repent Immediately and Ask God to Cleanse You of It

John said he wrote his First Epistle "so that you will not sin," but then added immediately, "if anybody does sin, we have one who speaks to the Father in our defense—Jesus Christ, the Righteous One" (1 John 2:1). "If we claim to be without sin, we deceive ourselves and the truth is not in us. If we confess our sins, he is faithful and just and will forgive us our sins and purify us from all unrighteousness" (1 John 1:8, 9).

I find this to be a wonderful provision. Suppose I am in the middle of a committee meeting somewhere and suddenly I realize that an evil thought has lodged in my mind. I don't need to debate with myself whether it was just a temptation, or whether I entertained it long enough that it became sin. It doesn't matter. I want it rooted out of my being. So I ask God to forgive me for having such thoughts and to cleanse me of them entirely. Then I am free to turn my thoughts and attention again toward the duty God has set before me.

This assuring counsel has encouraged me to repentance:

"As you see the enormity of sin, as you see yourself as you really are, do not give up to despair. It was sinners that Christ came to save. We have not to reconcile God to us, but—O wondrous love!—God in Christ is 'reconciling the world unto Himself.' 2 Corinthians 5:19. He is wooing by His tender love the hearts of His erring children. No earthly parent could be as patient with the faults and mistakes of his children, as is God with those He seeks to save. No one could plead more tenderly with the transgressor. No human lips ever poured out more tender entreaties to the wanderer than does He. All His promises, His warnings, are but the breathing of unutterable love.

"When Satan comes to tell you that you are a great sinner, look up to your Redeemer and talk of His merits. That which will help you is to look to His light. Acknowledge your sin, but tell the enemy that 'Christ Jesus came into the world to save sinners' and that you may be saved by His matchless love. 1 Timothy 1:15."[6]

Neil T. Anderson provides an illustration of how important this step is:

"Those of us who live in earthquake-prone southern California keep hearing about 'the big one,' which is thought by many to be inevitable along the San Andreas fault. Whenever we experience minor earthquakes (up to about four on the Richter scale), we may be frightened by them a bit, but we also see them as a good sign. These little temblors mean that the plates in the earth's crust beneath us are shifting. As long as the crust is adjusting this way it's unlikely that 'the big one' will hit. It's when we don't get any minor earthquakes for several months or years that the danger of a major, devastating quake increases.

"Living in the light, holding ourselves accountable to God, and confessing and dealing with sin on a daily basis prevents major spiritual crises from building up in our lives. If we keep saying, 'I don't have any sin,' or if we fail to acknowledge our shortcomings and settle our differences with people as God convicts us of them, we're in for 'the big one.' We will eventually lose our health, our family, our job, or our friendships. Unacknowledged sin is like a cancer that will grow to consume us."[7]

No matter how many times I may have asked forgiveness in the past for the same sin, I need to keep asking until complete victory is eventually gained. As C. S. Lewis said, "After each failure, ask forgiveness, pick yourself up, and try again. . . . The only fatal thing is to sit down content with anything less than perfection."[8]

4. Spend Quiet Time Getting to Know Jesus

In his book *To Know God,* Morris Venden has some highly practical and reassuring counsel for those of us who are ready to give up at times because of continuing sin in our lives over which we have not yet gained the victory:

"Is it possible to sin and know that you are sinning, and keep doing what you are doing wrong, and still be a Christian? How does Jesus treat sinners who sin?[9]

"He made His classic statement in Matthew 12:31: 'All manner of sin . . . shall be forgiven unto men.'. . . The only sin that would not be pardoned would be the one I don't ask pardon for, that I don't repent of. . . . Let's circle it in red and green and orange and purple that *'all manner of sin . . . shall be forgiven unto men,'* including known sin, including habitual sin, including persistent sin, including the worst of sins, such as pride."[10]

"So it is possible for the growing Christian to discover that he has a known sin going on in his life and at the same time a continuing relationship with Jesus."[11]

Then Venden makes this uncompromising observation: "As you study you see a further conclusion. Even though it is possible to have a relationship with God going on and a sin going on at the same time, sooner or later one or the other is going to go."[12]

"If you continue to know Jesus as your personal friend day by day, if you become meaningfully involved with Him in your private life, if nothing can take you from His side, then you will join John the Beloved in a transformation of character that will be unobtrusive, and imperceptible to you. But your friends will probably know it. And whatever sin you're struggling with, whether it's known or unknown, whether it's habitual or cherished or any of the other kinds, it will ultimately fade away."[13]

Ellen White gives the same assurance: "There are those who have known the pardoning love of Christ and who really desire to be children of God, yet they realize that their character is imperfect, their life faulty, and they are ready to doubt whether their hearts have been renewed by the Holy Spirit. To such I would say, Do not draw back in despair. We shall often have to bow down and weep at the feet of Jesus because of our shortcomings and mistakes, but we are not to be discouraged. Even if we are overcome by the enemy, we are not cast off, not forsaken and rejected of God. No;

Christ is at the right hand of God, who also maketh intercession for us. . . . Do not forget the words of Christ, 'The Father Himself loveth you.' John 16:27. He desires to restore you to Himself, to see His own purity and holiness reflected in you. And if you will but yield yourself to Him, He that hath begun a good work in you will carry it forward to the day of Jesus Christ." [14]

5. Rest in God

While repentance for our specific sins is important for gaining victory in spiritual warfare, Ellen White warns us against becoming preoccupied with our faults and weaknesses:

"It is Satan's constant effort to keep the attention diverted from the Saviour and thus prevent the union and communion of the soul with Christ. The pleasures of the world, life's cares and perplexities and sorrows, the faults of others, or your own faults and imperfections—to any or all of these he will seek to divert the mind. Do not be misled by his devices. Many who are really conscientious, and who desire to live for God, he too often leads to dwell upon their own faults and weaknesses, and thus by separating them from Christ he hopes to gain the victory. We should not make self the center and indulge anxiety and fear as to whether we shall be saved. All this turns the soul away from the Source of our strength. Commit the keeping of your soul to God, and trust in Him. Talk and think of Jesus. Let self be lost in Him. . . . Rest in God. He is able to keep that which you have committed to Him. If you will leave yourself in His hands, He will bring you off more than conqueror through Him that has loved you." [15]

An interesting prescription for the quiet agony of the continuing struggle against sin, is it not? Rest in God!

"In repentance and rest is your salvation, in quietness and trust is your strength" (Isa. 30:15).

"Listen to me, . . . you whom I have upheld since you were conceived, and have carried since your birth. Even to your old age and gray hairs I am he, I am he who will sustain you. I have made you and I will carry you; I will sustain you and I will rescue you" (Isa. 46:3, 4).

"My sheep listen to my voice; I know them, and they follow me. I give them eternal life, and they shall never perish; no one can snatch them out of my hand. My Father, who has given them to me, is greater than all; no one can snatch them out of my Father's hand" (John 10:27-29).

"He who began a good work in you will carry it on to completion until the day of Christ Jesus" (Phil. 1:6).

"Continue to work out your salvation with fear and trembling, for it is God who works in you to will and to act according to his good purpose" (Phil. 2:12, 13).

"I know whom I have believed, and am convinced that he is able to guard what I have entrusted to him for that day" (2 Tim. 1:12).

"The one who is in you is greater than the one who is in the world" (1 John 4:4).

"Do not be afraid or discouraged. . . . For the battle is not yours, but God's. . . . Go out to face them tomorrow, and the Lord will be with you" (2 Chron. 20:15, 17).

"The Lord will fight for you; you need only to be still" (Ex. 14:14).

---

[1] E. G. White, *The Acts of the Apostles,* pp. 314, 315.

[2] ———— , *Steps to Christ,* pp. 64, 65.

[3] *Ibid.,* p. 65.

[4] M. Moore, *The Crisis of the End Time,* p. 67.

[5] Neil T. Anderson, *The Bondage Breaker* (Eugene, Oreg.: Harvest House Publishers, 1990), pp. 138, 139.

[6] White, *Steps to Christ,* pp. 35, 36.

[7] Anderson, p. 156.

[8] C. S. Lewis, *Mere Christianity* (New York: MacMillan Pub. Co., Inc., 1960), pp. 93, 94.

[9] Morris Venden, *To Know God: A 5-Day Plan* (Washington, D.C.: Review and Herald Pub. Assn., 1983), p. 84.

[10] *Ibid.,* pp. 88, 89.

[11] *Ibid.,* p. 93.

[12] *Ibid.*

[13] *Ibid.,* p. 95.

[14] White, *Steps to Christ,* p. 64.

[15] *Ibid.,* pp. 71, 72.

CHAPTER TWELVE

The Ordinary Adventist Who Died in Church

Fortunately for the person who would have been involved, I couldn't find the illustration I was looking for to open this chapter. My good friend and colleague, Dwight K. Nelson, remembers the Sabbath one of his parishioners had a heart attack during the worship service and was taken right from the pew to the ambulance. But I couldn't find anyone who could remember being in a church service when someone actually died in the pew. Someone will no doubt send me the perfect illustration after this book is printed.

I'm writing this chapter because I believe it *is* happening every Sabbath (and in every church?)—members are dying a spiritual death while sitting in church singing hymns. Spiritual corpses occupy many a well-worn pew. I base this sobering assessment on Jesus' own words from His sermon on the mount: "Not everyone who says to me, 'Lord, Lord,' will enter the kingdom of heaven, but only he who does the will of my Father who is in heaven. Many will say to me on that day, 'Lord, Lord, did we not prophesy in your name, and in your name drive out demons and perform many miracles?' Then I will tell them plainly, 'I never knew you. Away from me, you evildoers!'" (Matt. 7:21-23). Jesus spoke those awesome words not to unchurched people, but to people who were apparently very active in the church.

I have to confess that I'm writing this chapter as much for

myself as for anyone else. I take Jesus' words to mean that I could be a regular church member, even be a minister and write a book, and still be missing something essential. Imagine after all these years finally being able to meet God face-to-face, only to hear Him say "Away from Me; I never knew you." I could hardly imagine anything worse, especially if I'd thought I'd been on the right track all along. I don't want that to happen to me or to anyone else if I can help it. That's the reason for this chapter.

It was Jesus Himself who revealed that the basis of our acceptance with God is rooted in the Father's heart that overflows with protective love and care for His children (Matt. 7:9-11). And it was Jesus Himself who assured us, "Whoever comes to me I will never drive away" (John 6:37). And yet it was this same Jesus who warned us that some who are active in church, and even achieving great accomplishments, are in spiritual peril and in jeopardy of losing everything. What are we to make of this awesome warning directed particularly to those in the church?

Hollow Religion

Some religion involves little more than ceremony. To the casual observer it may appear as the real thing. It may consist of regular church attendance, participation in some if not most of the other church meetings, giving of tithe, perhaps even holding a church office or two, etc. And to be complete, and true to the text, we'd have to throw in some prophesying, casting out demons, and performing of miracles, which would make it appear all the more like the real thing. But it would also have an emptiness and hollowness about it all. No sparkle in the eye. No joy. No delight. No real love. No spontaneous praise. No waking to the day with a song in the heart. No cup running over. No serendipitous encounters with Jesus through the day. No freshness. No intellectual stimulation from the devotional hour. No tears from new discoveries of God's greatness. No longing for the language to express the fullness one feels. No dreams of new accomplishments with God. No stretching beyond one's comfort zone to attempt something new for Him. No spiritual agony from intense battles with sin. No contagious enthusiasm. No eagerness to share the wonder of it all. Only duty and obligation, doing what one has to do, what one is supposed to do, what is required in order to inherit eternal life and to keep from being lost, settling into a habitual and comfortable pattern. Outwardly, and from a distance, the two types of religion may appear similar, but inwardly, where the feelings and emotions and very soul of the believer exist, they are worlds apart. One is life-giving, the other life-threatening, to the spiritual relationship.

Is there no value to doing right just because it is right, whether we feel like it or not? Yes, I believe there is, at least to start with. I may not feel like making a dietary change that I know would enable me to bring greater glory to God in my life but I am better off physically to make the change anyway, whether I feel like it or am enthused about it or not. If I really didn't want to tithe, would I be better off to do it anyway because it's a command? Perhaps. But it may also be in order for me to repent of my ungenerous spirit, for "God loves a cheerful giver" (2 Cor. 9:7).

A Dangerous Obedience

I used to think that disobeying the commandments was the ultimate manifestation of ungodliness—sexual immorality, allowing anything or anyone to come before God, experimenting with the occult, jealousy and discord in relationships, exclusive cliques that shut others out, lack of self-control, etc. The apostle Paul called such things the "works of the flesh" (Gal. 5:19, KJV). He warns that people who practice them will not inherit the kingdom of God (see verses 19-21). I can understand that and wholeheartedly affirm it.

But then one day I read how Paul evaluated his religious life before he found the real thing. He was born into a religious family who were members of the true religion. Educated in the best religious schools of his day, he became a religious leader and tried to live what he preached. When it came to keeping the commandments of God, he was "faultless." I wish I could say as much for myself. Paul was understandably content with his religion . . . until, that is, he discovered the real thing. Then he confessed that his religious experience up to that point, for all of its sterling pedigree, he now considered to be "rubbish," a complete "loss." All the while he thought he'd been living up to the requirements of God, he had actually been living "in the flesh" (Phil. 3:4-8).

That was the shocker for me. The very same words he used to characterize the rebellious disobedience of unbelievers—"in the flesh"—he now employed to characterize his own life of strict obedience before he found the real thing. Both were dangerous in their own right and if not remedied would result in spiritual death.

Born "Religious"

The reason that insight meant so much to me was that I was born "religious." From as early as I can remember I seemed to be attracted to religious things. Both my parents and grandparents have told me that I was generally an obedient child, albeit not without some needed spankings along the way, although I only remember getting two of them. As I grew older, I wasn't attracted to the crowd that ran around and got into trouble. I tended to associate with the church and its activities. Satan seemed to know that if he was going to get me, he'd have to do it inside the church, not outside. So that's where he went to work on me, just as he did with Paul. "Sin, seizing an opportunity in the commandment, deceived me and through it killed me" (Rom. 7:11, NRSV). And that's where he attacks a lot of us ordinary Adventists who are born, reared, and acculturated in the church, and never seemed to have seriously rebelled.

The Sinful Nature Bends Some Toward Religion

I've since learned that the sinful nature has two dominant expressions—irreligious behavior that wars against God and His commandments, and religious behavior that obeys the commandments as a way of appeasing God and securing our future. Sinful nature appears to bend some of us one way and some of us the other.

Many of us decry the irreligious bent, as if that were the most dangerous. But Jesus predominately attacked the prideful, self-righteous behavior that's rooted in the religious inclination of the sinful nature—the proud Pharisee who looked down on the repentant publican (Luke 18:9-14), the strict tithers who had unmerciful spirits (Matt. 23:23), etc. He called them "whitewashed tombs, which look beautiful on the outside but on the inside are full of dead men's bones and everything unclean. . . . On the outside you appear to people as righteous but on the inside you are full of hypocrisy and wickedness" (verses 27, 28).

I am in the class that Jesus hit the hardest. And while Jesus' most pointed warnings are to people like me, the religious bent of my sinful nature still tries to assure me that if I'm religious enough, if I just keep doing the things I know are right and avoiding the things I know are wrong, then that's all that's really necessary, and I don't need whatever it is that Jesus called people like me to experience. So the naturally religious types, like me, can become corpses in the pew without even realizing what's happening to us.

The Real Thing

So, what is the "real thing" that Jesus wanted the "good" people like myself to experience. What is the experience that Paul found that made him consider his previous religious life to be a complete "loss"? Obviously, it's not something that's never been known before, as if God were waiting all these centuries for my book to come out to disclose it. As John said, "I am not writing you a new command but an old one, which you have had since the beginning" (1 John 2:7). But he also acknowledged, "Yet I am writing you a new command" in the sense that many of his readers had not yet experienced the very thing that God had called them to live out from the beginning (verse 8).

The "real thing" is simply this: Connecting with God through Jesus Christ in a genuine love relationship. And it's been with us from the beginning: "Love the Lord your God with all your heart and with all your soul and with all your strength" (Deut. 6:5; cf. Matt. 22:37, 38). "Only the service of love can be acceptable to God."[1]

A religious experience not characterized by genuine love for God is religious formalism. Obedience to God's commandments outside the context of that love is mere dutiful compliance motivated by fear of what will happen to us if we don't. If God would have been satisfied for His creatures to have this kind of experience, He could have either tortured Lucifer into submission or killed him at the first sign of his disaffection, and the remaining angels would have obeyed Him from then on out of fear of what would happen to them if they didn't. But genuine love produces an entirely different motivation and experience. "There is no fear in love. But perfect love drives out fear, because fear has to do with punishment. The one who fears is not made perfect in love" (1 John 4:18). God knows that our ultimate happiness depends upon that love. So He requires it of us, and offers it to us, now.

No Small Distinction

Make no mistake about it: there's a world of difference between serving God from fear of what will happen if we don't and for the reward we will receive if we do, and serving God in the joy and delight that comes from a genuine love for God. It's the difference between enjoying our experience with God and enduring it. Also it's the fundamental contrast between a religious experience that nourishes spiritual life, and one that can literally destroy it. God has not called us to be slaves who serve Him from fear, but children who relate to Him in love. "For you did not receive a spirit that makes you a slave again to fear, but you received the Spirit of sonship. And by him [Jesus] we cry, '*Abba,* Father'" (Rom. 8:15).

Paul, once driven by an in-the-flesh compulsion for religious exactitude, found a new and even more powerful motivating force—"Christ's love compels us" (2 Cor. 5:14). This transformation didn't lead him to become any less active for God, but it was a new experience altogether, one that made everything before it seem like "rubbish."

Ken McFarland's parable "Metamorphosis" illustrates this distinction. Heather Hathaway was a housekeeper with a tyrant for an employer. Not only did she hate her work—scrubbing floors on hands and knees, washing heavy pots and pans, chopping wood for the cookstove, laboring long at the washboard—but she received a mere pittance of a wage. Yet she did her work because she was afraid of becoming even more impoverished if she didn't.

One day her boss beat her for tardiness and threw her out onto the street, jobless. John Manchester, a wealthy businessman, found her, had her nursed back to health, and gave her a housekeeping job on his own estate. The sizable increase in her pay made her life lighter, but she still intensely disliked her work—scrubbing floors on hands and knees, washing heavy pots and pans, etc. It was drudgery.

As good stories go, John Manchester, also a handsome bachelor, fell in love with Heather and she with him. After the wedding he wanted to hire someone to do the housekeeping, but she would have none of it. The chores that had once galled her now delighted her. She even wanted to do more. Love had made all the difference.[2]

At the end of his parable, McFarland concludes with this statement from *Steps to Christ:*

There are those who "seek to perform the duties of the Christian life as that which God requires of them in order to gain heaven. Such religion is worth nothing. When Christ dwells in the heart, the soul will be so filled with his love . . . that it will cleave to Him. Love to

Christ will be the spring of action. . . . A profession of Christ without this deep love is mere talk, dry formality, and heavy drudgery."[3]

Meanwhile, Back at My Own Journey

For many years of my Christian experience I didn't have that kind of love for God. I used the right language, but I didn't have the experience to go with it. The worst of it was, I didn't even know that true religion was anything other than what I was experiencing. However, I believe God accepted me while in that condition, because it was the only kind of religion I knew.

Then sometime in 1972, during my pastorate in Las Vegas, God gently directed me to an awareness of something more in the spiritual relationship than I was experiencing. I began searching for something to fill this new spiritual hunger that had awakened within me. In the process God led me to the realization that I didn't really love Him. Perhaps He had tried to alert me to this reality previously, and I had simply denied it or ignored His promptings. But this time I couldn't run away from it. I knew within myself that I did not love God. I didn't hate Him or dislike Him, but I also knew that I didn't love Him either.

I didn't know what to do with this disturbing revelation. So I did the only thing I could think to do—I prayed about it. As I remember, it was a most awkward prayer that went something like this: "Dear God, I don't know exactly how to say this or how to talk to You about it, but I'm beginning to realize that I don't love You, in spite of the many hundreds of times I've told You I do. I don't even know what it means to love You. I don't know what to do about this, but I realize that it matters to me, and that I want to learn to love You. Would You help me?"

Nothing happened.

After a few weeks of praying that prayer, I began to search on my own for something that would fill the void I was feeling. At our fall ministers' meeting, I asked my conference president, Dan Dirksen, to lay His hands on me and pray that I would receive the Holy Spirit, as they used to do in the New Testament. He had all the ministers of the conference gather around and pray for me.

Still nothing happened.

Secretly I began to attend some charismatic meetings, looking for someone I could trust to lay hands on me so I could get instant gratification for my spiritual hunger. But the books I read on that subject and the things I saw happen at the meetings I attended made me extremely uncomfortable and steered me away from taking that approach.

Finally I went to see H.M.S. Richards in his private study behind his home in Los Angeles. He spent a couple hours with me and prayed for me. But he also told me that I would find no shortcuts to filling my spiritual hunger. It would come in God's way through prayer and the study of His Word.

I can't tell you exactly when or where it happened. Looking back on it, I believe H.M.S. Richards was right. I did try to be more faithful in devotional study and prayer, seeking God. And over time, a period of several years actually, I came to love Him. I didn't wake up one day with that experience, but I knew when love for God had begun to change my whole outlook on life and religion. I hadn't realized that I'd had any fear of God until love for Him gradually began to replace it.

A quantum leap in this experience came for me during a six-month period when I made a special devotional study of the events surrounding the crucifixion of Jesus. I came out of that experience with a love, a respect, an admiration for God that has endeared Him to me as nothing else ever had before. He is without doubt the most exciting and interesting and neatest Person I've ever known.

I wish I could say that I feel forever delivered from the danger of becoming a corpse in the pew or, God forbid, a corpse in the pulpit. But I know my heart all too well. I cannot trust myself even a single day without spending time seeking God and enjoying Him in moments of devotional study and prayer. I still have intense struggles with my sinful nature and still feel very self-righteous at times. God has a long way to go with me in many areas. But I also have great confidence in what He can do. And He has taught me that He is able to keep that which I have committed to Him—namely, my eternal salvation and spiritual growth unto sanctification—for that day (2 Tim. 1:12).

Principles Designed to Keep Us From Dying in Church

To anyone who recognizes that his or her sinful nature is bent toward religious formalism as mine is, I invite you to consider the following principles that my experience has taught me can keep us from dying in church:

1. Recognize That You Cannot Generate a Genuine Love for God in Your Own Heart—It Is a Gift From God

Paul, who experienced this love, testified, "God has poured out his love into our hearts by the Holy Spirit whom he has given us" (Rom. 5:5).

Ask God to deliver you from a dry, formal religion, and to give you the real thing (Matt. 7:7). Tell God that you don't want to merely settle for the "right religion," you want a relationship with Him that will enable you to say with David and with Jesus, "I delight to do your will, O my God" (Ps. 40:8).

2. Determine to Make No Entanglements of the Heart That You Know Would Compromise Your Relationship With God

God will alert you to the blockages in your life that prevent Him from drawing you deeper into His love. When God gives you such a revelation, He does not do so as a judge rendering a verdict and sentencing, but as a skillful physician offering a precise diagnosis and prescription for healing. Any wounds made in the process we can compare to incisions from a lifesaving surgery. As God reveals such things to you, repent of them and ask Him to cleanse you.

Recently I was praying the prayer of David: "Search me, O God, and know my heart; test me and know my anxious thoughts. See if there is any offensive way in me, and lead me in the way everlasting" (Ps. 139:23, 24). About that time Lyn happened to mention to me that I sometimes came away from my devotional periods with a judgmental attitude toward her and the children. Her analysis didn't exactly make my day. But then I realized that, through Lyn, God was answering my prayer to make known any offense in me that is preventing me from experiencing His love more fully. Knowing that I do not want to be a judgmental person, He has given me a new subject matter for prayer—again! And I believe that as I lift this up before Him and seek to be a more accepting person, He will make the difference that both He and I (as well as Lyn and the children) want in my life.

3. Seek to Know God Through Jesus

This is how a love for God grows. Some people are so attractive and interesting and trustworthy that when you really get to know them you can hardly help but love them. I've discovered God to be just such a person.

When Paul recounted his conversion from religious formalism to the real thing, he described it this way: "Whatever was to my profit I now consider loss for the sake of Christ. What is more, I consider everything a loss compared to the surpassing greatness of knowing Christ Jesus my Lord" (Phil. 3:7, 8). "The surpassing greatness of knowing Christ Jesus" was in sharp contrast to all the religious activities he had been involved in before.

There really is a "surpassing greatness" in getting to know Jesus through daily devotional study and prayer. It is the spring from which the river of true spirituality flows. If anything at all dams up this spring, the result is inevitable—spiritual death no matter how often one occupies a pew, or a pulpit. But it's also true that if you drink from this spring regularly, new spiritual life is equally inevitable.

A favorite poster of mine hangs on a wall in my office. A 12-year-old boy who had been failing in school and to whom I had become a big brother of sorts gave it to me. His father had deserted him, and I was apart from my own children for much of that time. So we were a good match. We hiked, bowled, played games, and read together. He even made pastoral visits with me. Soon he was doing better in school, and even got an after-school job. At Christmas he gave me the poster. It's a picture of a mare and her colt standing side by side, looking identical except for their sizes. Underneath the caption reads, "We grow in the image of those we love."

As I understand it, the spiritual relationship works the same way.

4. Share the Love You've Experienced

Spiritual death is only a matter of time unless you eventually get out into the world to share the love you have been seeking for yourself. But now I'm already delving into bottom-line religion, the subject of our next chapter.

---

[1] E. G. White, *Patriarchs and Prophets* (Mountain View, Calif.: Pacific Press Pub. Assn., 1890), p. 42.

[2] Ken McFarland, *Garland Showdown* (Mountain View, Calif.: Pacific Press Pub. Assn., 1981), pp. 10-13.

[3] White, *Steps to Christ,* pp. 44, 45.

LOOKING OUT AT THE WORLD

LOVE

PRAY

witness

share

CHAPTER THIRTEEN

Bottom-line Religion

During a routine visit to my office one day, a parishioner's comment provided a clue for a spiritual quest I had been on for months. I had been seeking for the most important thing God wants from me in my spiritual relationship. But first let me go back to the beginning of the story.

In previous chapters I've shared with you much of my spiritual journey in discovering the security of God's parental love and of having a corresponding love awakened within my own heart. At a certain point in that journey I felt a strong need to know where to go from there. What was the most important thing for me to be doing, in terms of my spiritual relationship? What is the bottom line of the spiritual relationship? What would God like most from me?

Options for the Bottom Line

As I began to search for an answer, I discovered many options. I've distilled them here to a list of 10. At one point or another in my quest I considered each of these as a serious contender for being religion's bottom line.

1. Personal Happiness

I heard a presentation that suggested the chief end of life is to live a well-balanced, well-rounded existence that brings the most personal satisfaction and happiness. The presenter cited

Ecclesiastes 3:12, 13: "I know that there is nothing better for them than to be happy and enjoy themselves as long as they live; moreover, it is God's gift that all should eat and drink and take pleasure in all their toil" (NRSV). If a person can do well in school, eventually get a good job, have a happy family, reap the fruitage of honest labor, enjoy the wonders of God's natural world, cultivate wholesome relationships with God and others, learning to be happy and content in these things, is this not the very kind of life God originally placed us on this earth for?

2. Being Saved

The well-known story in Acts 16 highlighted the important question "What must I do to be saved?" (verse 30). Should not pursuing the answer to this great question be the ultimate priority of life? Even for those of us who have already become Christians, should we not discover those things that could jeopardize our salvation and attend to them? What could possibly be a more important focus in life than this?

3. Knowing God

Jesus said, "This is eternal life: that they may know you, the only true God, and Jesus Christ, whom you have sent" (John 17:3). When Martha expressed concern about all the things she felt she needed to be doing, Jesus tried to put her heart at rest by telling her, "Only one thing is needed"—namely, sitting at His feet in an effort to get to know Him better (Luke 10:42). What could possibly be more important than this, especially when Jesus Himself said that getting to know God and Jesus is the "one thing" needed, and is what eternal life is all about?

4. Praying

A number of persuasive Christian books identify prayer as the chief priority for the Christian. Jesus said, "Ask and it will be given to you" (Matt. 7:7). James says that we don't realize more than we do in our spiritual lives because we don't ask God for more than we do (James 4:2). We have heard the story of Martin Luther who at times spent four hours a day in prayer. Perhaps, more than anything else, God wants us to be spending more time in prayer with Him.

5. Understanding Scripture

Paul said that all Scripture was inspired by God in part that we might understand true doctrine (2 Tim. 3:16, KJV). Should the primary focus of the Christian life be to "know our Bibles," to achieve an understanding of true doctrine and last-day prophecies, and how they relate to our daily lives? Have we not been warned, "None but those who have fortified the mind with the truths of the Bible will stand through the last great conflict"?[1]

6. Worship

The book of Revelation portrays numerous scenes of earthly and heavenly beings in the act of worshiping God. The first angel's message calls the last generation on earth to "worship him who made the heavens, the earth, the sea and the springs of water" (Rev. 14:7). Jesus says the Father seeks for true worshipers who worship in spirit and truth (John 4:23). Perhaps the chief focus for last-day Christians ought to be learning to worship God with more purity and spiritual depth.

7. Loving Service

James said that pure religion involves helping the fatherless and widows in their afflictions (James 1:27). Does making a commitment to help people constitute the bottom-line principle of the Christian life?

8. Abstaining From Worldliness

In the text just cited, James also says pure religion involves keeping "oneself from being polluted by the world." John wrote, "Do not love the world or anything in the world. . . . For everything in the world—the cravings of sinful man, the lust of his eyes and the boasting of what he has and does—comes not from the Father but from the world" (1 John 2:15, 16). Should the chief focus of the Christian be to achieve purity of life in contrast to the corruption around us?

9. Character Perfection

Jesus called us to "be perfect, therefore, as your heavenly Father is perfect" (Matt. 5:48). Should the primary focus of the Christian be to obtain perfection of Christian character? Especially in light of such statements as this: "When the character of Christ shall be perfectly reproduced in His people, then He will come to claim them as His own."[2]

10. Seeking the Spirit

Before Jesus ascended to heaven, He told His disciples to wait in Jerusalem until they received the Holy Spirit, and only after they were so empowered should they then engage in ministry on His behalf (Acts 1:4, 5). Should not Christians concentrate on tarrying in the private chamber of prayer, pleading to the Father for the latter-rain outpouring of the Holy Spirit and its accompanying empowerment to live godly lives and finish our work on this earth so we can go home to heaven with Him?

To be complete, this list may need to be longer. But even as is, it was formidable enough for me. How was I to determine which, if any, of these great Christian principles and admonitions constituted the overriding Christian priority to which all the others were subservient and to which they ministered? Or was I on the wrong track even to be searching for such a bottom-line Christian principle for my life?

The Visit That Provided the Needed Clue

While I was in the midst of trying to answer these questions, I received a call from a church member who wanted to talk to me. She phoned on the prayer meeting day, so I arranged to meet her at the church an hour before the meeting. Although I expected her to relay some personal problem for which she wanted counseling, what actually unfolded, however, was a most beautiful testimony of how God had been working in her life over the past couple years.

An episode of her testimony seemed to relate directly to the question I was wrestling with. As she related it, I felt that God was giving me direction for my search. It was so important that I asked her to repeat it for me several times so I could write it down just as she related it. This is what she said:

"At one point in my Christian experience I began to pray and pray for the Holy Spirit to come upon me. And then I waited and waited for something to happen. I didn't really know what to expect or what it would be like, but I felt that when it happened I would know it for sure, and so I kept on praying for it. Then one day I began to be impressed that I needed to get involved and start reaching out to others, and that the gift of the Holy Spirit was received by doing something with what I already had. The Holy Spirit would then be with me in greater measure as I sensed my need for Him, and would make my ministry for others more effective."

For the next several months I scrutinized her testimony in light of Scripture. This is what I found.

The Essence of the Gospel

At one time someone asked Jesus point-blank what was the greatest issue of life, "the greatest commandment in the Law"—the bottom line, if you please (Matt. 22:36). What made the incident so significant was the fact that Jesus often received questions to which He did not give a direct answer, perhaps because the questioners were insincere, or because the questions themselves were the wrong ones as far as the ultimate issues of life are concerned. But when asked about God's highest priority for us, Jesus jumped on it as though He had been waiting for it for a long time.

"Jesus replied: 'Love the Lord your God with all your heart and with all your soul and with all your mind.' This is the first and greatest commandment. And the second is like it: 'Love your neighbor as yourself.' All the Law and the Prophets hang on these two commandments" (Matt. 22:37-40).

In other words, Jesus distilled the entire message of God through the prophets of old to these two commands to love God and one another.

Yes, but does this really help? Love means so many different things to different people. Much transpires in the name of love that is cheap and even destructive.

True. But the kind of love Jesus identified as the ultimate priority of life is not romanticism or emotional sentimentality. It is a commitment to help others who need us, in ways that are healing and sometimes very costly.

In what most theologians would agree is the greatest sermon ever preached, the Sermon on the Mount, Jesus compressed God's revelation to humanity into a single sentence that expresses in the most practical of terms what love is about: "In everything, do to others what you would have them do to you, for this sums up the Law and the Prophets" (Matt. 7:12).

The Spanish have a simple chorus that captures this sentiment. It goes:

> "Amor, amor, amor, amor,
> La esencia del Evangelio es amor.
> Ama a tu prójimo como a ti mismo,
> Amor, amor, amor."

Which, being interpreted for Spanish illiterates like myself, means:

> "Love, love, love, love,
> The essence of the good news is love.
> Love your neighbor as yourself,
> Love, love, love."

The essence of the good news? The essence of the gospel? The bottom line of the Christian life? To treat other people as we would want to be treated ourselves if we were in their place? Is that possible? I used to think that was kindergarten material. We sang it in my kindergarten class when I was a boy: "I have two dollies and I am glad, you have no dollies and that's too bad. I'll share my dollies, for I love you. And that's what Jesus wants me to do." And somehow even as a young boy I was able to get through the feminist language of that simple verse. Instinctively I knew that it had something to do with my two baseballs, or two toy trucks, or something else that one of my friends had none of. I sensed that Jesus was asking me to think of how I would feel if I had none of those things, and to share with someone who didn't. That's pretty heavy stuff for a little ordinary Adventist boy. And it's even heavier for the ordinary Adventist adult that I am today, for my adult toys are a lot more expensive, more private, more hard earned (at least by me) than my child's toys were.

John said it this way: "Let us not love with words or tongue but with actions and in truth" (1 John 3:18). "If anyone has material possessions and sees his brother in need but has no pity on him, how can the love of God be in him?" (verse 17).

Humanism? Or Antidote for Its Counterpart?

I had a hard time accepting this at first. It sounded too unspiritual, almost humanistic. Is that all religion is, just living by the golden rule?

Of course not. But if we think we're religious and we're not living by the golden rule, we're missing the point entirely. Love as practically expressed in the golden rule is the bottom line of the spiritual life.

If godless humanism is the fatal ditch on the left side of life's highway, perhaps the corresponding ditch on the right would be a religion that's exclusively vertical in its focus. Is this not the message of 1 John 4:20: "If anyone says 'I love God [the vertical level of religion],' yet hates his brother [the horizontal level], he is a liar. For anyone who does not love his brother, whom he has seen [the horizontal level], cannot love God, whom he has not seen [the vertical level]"? There is no such thing as genuine love for God without a corresponding love for others.

The Greatest of These

If there's one chapter in the Bible that's referred to more than any other as the love chapter it would have to be 1 Corinthians 13. This chapter says that we may have great possessions or great wealth, we may have great faith and powerful spiritual gifts, but it all counts for nothing if we do not relate toward others who need us with a practical love that helps and heals. Then the chapter describes love by providing a list of attitudes and actions that support and bless people.

First Corinthians 13 then ends with this remarkable statement: "And now these three remain: faith, hope and love. But the greatest of these is love" (verse 13).

"These three remain: faith, hope and love." I take "faith" in this context to pertain to all things that have to do with cultivating the relationship with God and developing trust in God—of approaching life and living one's life from the standpoint that life's highest priority is to develop a relationship with God. Next I interpret "hope" to pertain to all things that have to do with personal salvation and eternal life—of approaching life and living life from the standpoint that life's highest priority is to gain personal salvation. And I interpret Paul's use of "love" here to pertain to acts of compassion and concern toward those in need; approaching life and living life from the standpoint that the governing principle in the life of a Christian is actually doing things that bring the greatest possible help and blessing to people who need us. And while Paul says that faith, hope, and love will always be important for the Christian, he did not want the truth to be lost that one of them was the greatest, the bottom-line principle—"But the greatest of these is love."

Ellen White made the same point in one of her discussions regarding the divine remedies for the serious spiritual illnesses of the Laodicean church as described in Revelation 3. Concerning Christ's prescription that His people buy gold from Him, she wrote: "The gold mentioned by Christ, the True Witness, which all must have, has been shown . . . to be faith and love combined, and love takes the precedence of faith."[3]

Love's Walking Shoes

Jesus illustrated genuine love in the famous story recorded in Luke 10. This incident is remarkably similar in many ways to the one in Matthew 22 that I referred to earlier. But it also contains some very helpful and instructive differences.

The story begins with an expert in the law confronting Jesus with what he considered to be the ultimate issue in life: "'Teacher,' he asked, 'what must I do to inherit eternal life?'" (verse 25). Instead of answering the question outright, as He had done to the questioner in Matthew 22, Jesus treated it as if it were the wrong question in terms of life's ultimate priority. Note how His skillful question turned the discussion around to focus on the bottom-line issue:

"'What is written in the Law?' he replied. 'How do you read it?' He [the expert in the law] answered: '"Love the Lord your God with all your heart and with all your soul and with all your strength and with all your mind"; and, "Love your neighbor as yourself."' 'You have answered correctly,' Jesus replied. 'Do this and you will live'" (verses 26-28).

Evidently this man already knew the heart of the matter, or perhaps he had studied up on Jesus' teachings and merely repeated the answer he knew Jesus wanted. It's not so hard to give the right answer sometimes, is it? I learned the great commandment by memory many years ago. The hard part for me was recognizing how to integrate it into my life, how to give the great commandment its rightful place in my hierarchy of values, how to put on its walking shoes.

The expert in the law had the right answer, but he too had found it difficult to integrate into his life. Out of frustration he shot back the sarcastic question Just how far does God expect us to take this neighbor thing? (verse 29). In answer, and to illustrate the true spirit of the commandment, Jesus told the story of a man who on his way to Jericho fell victim to thieves, was beaten and left for dead; and about the priest and the Levite who passed him by. And then there came the Samaritan, whom the priest, the Levite, and the wounded man—all three—considered the scum of the earth. He alone stopped to administer CPR, and provided for the wounded man's long-term care.

Then Jesus came to the punch line of the story, which He elicited in part from the skeptical questioner himself:

" 'Which of these three do you think was a neighbor to the man who fell into the hands of robbers?' The expert in the law replied, 'The one who had mercy on him.' Jesus told him, 'Go and do likewise' " (verses 36, 37).

That response marked the end of my quest for the direction that my spiritual focus should take. I found myself back in kindergarten class with Jesus' words echoing in my ears, "Go and do likewise."

Bottom-line Options Revisited

But where does this leave the remaining principles and admonitions on my original list? Is their value and place in the Christian life compromised by their subordinate position to the great commandment and the golden rule?

I can answer that question only with my own testimony that this understanding has enhanced the value and place of the other components of the Christian life for me, albeit in a new perspective.

1. Happiness

It's admirable to live a well-balanced life, to enjoy one's work, family, and friends. But life itself teaches us that the deepest and most lasting happiness comes not through seeking it as an end in itself, but as a by-product of living one's life in love for God through helpful acts toward others.

2. Being Saved

The question "What must I do to be saved?" is the most important question one can ask before coming to God. But if everything we do as Christians results only because we think it will contribute in some way toward our own personal salvation, then the Christian life could become the most selfish of all lifestyles.

3. Knowing God

How about the "only one thing" that "is needed"—knowing God and Jesus—which Jesus Himself said was eternal life (Luke 10:42; John 17:3)? The importance of knowing God is every bit as vital as Jesus said it was. But we must never limit knowing God to a strictly cerebral exercise of learning about God. Note how the Scriptures expand our understanding of what it means to know God: "'He defended the cause of the poor and needy, and so all went well. Is that not what it means to know me?' declares the Lord" (Jer. 22:16). What is the "one thing" that "is needed" needed for? Is it not required as the divine enablement for fulfilling the great commandment and golden rule? Not exclusively, perhaps, but primarily?

4. Praying

Even the life of study and prayer for the purpose of having a relationship with God will fail if it becomes an end in itself. Morris Vendon says, "In nine cases out of 10, if there has been a time of meaningful communication with God day by day but it has gone sour, it is because of a lack of involvement in outreach and service and sharing with others."[4] It's for sure that we can have no ultimately effective service for others and witness for God apart from a growing, personal relationship with Him. "This spirit [of service and witness] is the sure outgrowth of a soul truly converted."[5] And it's equally true that any spiritual revival or relationship with God that does not go deep enough to result in a life of service to others will not last.

Note this statement from *Steps to Christ:* "The only [primary?] way to grow in grace [in our relationship with God, toward perfection of Christian character?] is to be disinterestedly doing the very work which Christ has enjoined upon us—to engage, to the extent of our ability, in helping and blessing those who need the help we can give them."[6] "Those who thus become participants in labors of love are brought nearest to their Creator."[7]

5. Understanding Scripture

We cannot discount the importance of knowing the Scriptures in these last days. From outside the church, from its fringes, and unfortunately, even from within, many voices claim to have the one understanding of Scripture that all must have who would be saved. And Jesus gave clear warning that such claims will increase in intensity and deception as the final day nears (Matt. 24:23, 24). Could it be anything but presumption to neglect the study of the Scriptures at such a time as this? But none could quote Scripture better than those who instigated the crucifixion of Jesus. Knowing what the Bible says is not in and of itself a guarantee of salvation or of a life of usefulness.

6. Worship

Worship can never be divorced from service and still be acceptable to God. God rejected the worship of a nation that failed to "seek justice, encourage the oppressed. Defend the cause of the fatherless, plead the case of the widow" (Isa. 1:10-17). Jesus said: "If you are offering your gift at the altar [worshiping on the vertical level] and there remember that your brother [or sister] has something against you [an estrangement on the horizontal level], leave your gift there in front of the altar. First go and be reconciled to your brother [the horizontal dimension of worship]; then come and offer your gift [the vertical dimension of our worship]" (Matt. 5:23, 24).

7. Loving Service

James's definition of true religion as loving service to others in need is religion's bottom line (James 1:27). This quality of love for others, which leads to serving others in ways that we ourselves would want to be treated, seemed to be the quality that was missing from those who opposed Jesus when He came (Matt. 23:1-4). It was the one quality He specifically noted would be determinative in the final judgment (Matt. 25:31-46).

8. Abstaining From Worldliness

James's inclusion of purity of life, in contrast to the corruption dominant in the world, in his definition of true religion reminds us of Jesus' prayer for His disciples that though they would be *in* the world (to serve it), they might not be *of* the world (participating in its evil practices) (James 1:27; John 17:14-18). Here again, purity of life seems not to be an end in itself, but a qualification for most effectively representing God in one's service to others.

9. Character Perfection

In context, Ellen White's statement that Christ is waiting to return until His character is perfectly reproduced in His children is said to be fulfilled when His children manifest "the Spirit of unselfish love and labor for others."[8] Elsewhere she describes a person who possesses "the religion of Christ" and "the character of Christ" as one who "becomes unselfish." One who "becomes upright, so that it is second nature to him to do to others as he would have others do to him."[9] Note also: "The completeness [perfection?] of Christian character is attained when the impulse to help and bless others springs constantly from within."[10]

10. Seeking the Spirit

When the Holy Spirit comes into the life, empowerment for witness and service takes place. Garrie Williams quotes Acts 1:8, then adds: "Witness or service is the primary and paramount reason for the outpouring of the Holy Spirit. All other reasons find their ultimate purpose in this."[11] Communion with the Holy Spirit tunes our senses to the still small voice that guides us to act wisely and compassionately at appropriate times and in appropriate ways in our service and witness.

Living the Bottom Line

The Adventist Church is no stranger to the bottom-line principle. In her most comprehensive mission statement, Ellen White wrote: "To take people right where they are, whatever their position or condition, and help them in every way possible—this is gospel ministry."[12]

When Seventh-day Adventists were few in number they began an educational system, a medical ministry, and a disaster relief program that today reaches around the world and offers educational opportunities, medical treatment, and disaster relief to hundreds of thousands of people in the impoverished developing countries of the world as well as the developed countries. Every loaf of bread delivered, every Breathe-Free stop-smoking seminar conducted, every cooking school, every stress seminar, every parenting class, every grief seminar, every Bible study, every evangelistic series can be an extension of the bottom-line principle into the community.

The corporate ministries of the church are not more important than the many daily, unheralded acts of courtesy and kindness performed by members to family, friends, work associates, and varied acquaintances. Indeed, we have been assured that "if we would humble ourselves before God, and be kind and courteous and tenderhearted and pitiful [empathetic], there would be one hundred conversions to the truth where now there is only one."[13]

---

[1] E. G. White, *The Great Controversy,* pp. 593, 594.
[2] ———— , *Christ's Object Lessons,* p. 69.
[3] ———— , *Testimonies,* vol. 2, p. 36.
[4] Venden, *To Know God,* p. 70.
[5] White, *Steps to Christ,* p. 78.
[6] *Ibid.,* p. 80.
[7] *Ibid.,* p. 79.
[8] ———— , *Christ's Object Lessons,* pp. 68, 69.
[9] ———— , *Our Father Cares,* p. 17.
[10] ———— , *The Acts of the Apostles,* p. 551.
[11] Garrie F. Williams, *How to Be Filled With the Holy Spirit and Know It* (Hagerstown, Md.: Review and Herald Pub. Assn., 1991), p. 90.
[12] White, *Testimonies,* vol. 6, p. 301.
[13] *Ibid.,* vol. 9, p. 189.

CHAPTER FOURTEEN

Witnessing Bloopers

Videos of sports bloopers feature the major blunders of sports heroes whose embarrassing mistakes often ended up aiding the opposing side. Some church members have felt similarly about the attempts they've made to witness, attempts that not only felt embarrassingly awkward to themselves but also seemed to turn those they were witnessing to away from Christ rather than to attract them to Him.

Some members who have attempted, unsuccessfully, to witness in the past have thereby concluded that "evangelism" isn't their spiritual gift and have tried to suppress the desire or sense of responsibility to witness to others directly about Christ. Yet even many of them feel convicted at times that they could be doing more than they are to witness for Christ. That conviction can be most disturbing when one doesn't know exactly how to go about it. This chapter seeks to meet that need—to serve as an ordinary Adventist's guide to effective witnessing.

Bottom-line Religion's Bottom Line

How would you feel about a doctor who treated a smoker's cough with cough medicine only, or who used Maalox to treat a patient with stomach discomfort who died shortly thereafter of stomach cancer? Would you go to a doctor who had earned the reputation of treating symptoms instead of finding the cause of the disease? When people went to Jesus, the Great Physician, with their felt needs, He ministered to them at that level, but He constantly had their ultimate need in mind—their spiritual need. "The Saviour mingled with men as one who desired their good. He showed His sympathy for them, ministered to their needs, and won their confidence. Then He bade them, 'Follow Me.'"[1]

When we take a loaf of bread to the neighbors, when we help people stop smoking or drinking or enable them to handle a life crisis, when we take the time to listen to someone going through the heartache of divorce or bereavement, we minister to them and bless them. But bottom-line religion that does unto others as we would want them to do for us were we in their place does not rest satisfied until we have introduced those we care about to Him whom to know is life abundant and life eternal. Bottom-line religion means "teaching them to obey everything I have commanded you," as Jesus empowered us to do (Matt. 28:20).

Christian witnessing isn't just for those few especially endowed with the gift of evangelism. It's the ultimate expression of anyone who's committed to bottom-line religion. Jesus told His followers from all walks of life: "You are the salt of the earth. . . . You are the light of the world. . . . Let your light shine before others, so that they may see your good works and give glory to your Father in heaven" (Matt. 5:13-16, NRSV). In his general letter to all Christians, James wrote, "Whoever turns a sinner from the error of his way will save him from death and cover over a multitude of sins" (James 5:20).

The impulse to speak to others about Jesus comes naturally to someone who is having a daily experience with Him. We talk to people about things we're excited about—falling in love, a new baby or grandchild, even a new car or bread machine. If Jesus is more wonderful than any of these, doesn't it make sense that we would want to tell others about Him? "No sooner does one come to Christ than there is born in his heart a desire to make known to others what a precious friend he has found in Jesus; the saving and sanctifying truth cannot be shut up in his heart. If we are clothed with the righteousness of Christ and are filled with the joy of His indwelling Spirit we shall not be able to hold our peace."[2] To keep from witnessing, a vibrant Christian would have to "quench" the Spirit, which Paul instructed us not to do (1 Thess. 5:19, KJV).

If It's So Natural, Why Is It So Hard?

Yet some of us who genuinely love God still find it hard to witness for Him. Why is this?

For one thing, when we have a new job or new spouse, new babies and grandchildren, people tend to ask us about those things. When was the last time someone asked you to describe your relationship with Jesus? Also, we live in an age when some consider it to be socially inappropriate to initiate a conversation about spiritual things. The familiar taboo against discussing politics or religion seems to hold even more true for religion than for politics. In the post-David Koresh era some people may seem even more skittish when approached about spiritual things.

Note the apostle John's explanation of why he and the other apostles wrote about Christ and the Christian experience as much as they did: "We write this to make our joy complete" (1 John 1:4). No Christian's joy is complete until he or she is sharing Jesus with others in some way.

Seven Principles for Successful Witnessing

How can you witness in a way that attracts people to Jesus and His truth, rather than causing them to shy away from it? How can you keep your witnessing experience from being an endless series of embarrassing bloopers?

Over the years I have certainly made more than my share of witnessing bloopers. But I felt compelled to keep trying again and again until I began to see people accepting Christ and becoming members of His church on a regular basis. Along the way I've discovered seven fundamental principles of witnessing that have made the difference for me.

1. Make your own calling and election sure (2 Peter 1:10). Perhaps it should just go without saying that unless you have an experience with Jesus yourself, your witnessing experience will be extremely disappointing. It's just too important, however, to ignore.

We know, of course, that some people have come to faith in Christ from the preaching of an evangelist later discovered to have been having an adulterous affair at the time. The apostle Paul was aware of so-called Christians in his day who taught about Christ out of "envy and rivalry" and "selfish ambition," seeking to upstage Paul; yet he was confident that even such an impurely motivated witness for Christ could still make a saving difference to the hearers (Phil. 1:15-18). That assures me that God can still use me for His glory even though I am far from perfect.

But Jesus rebuked hypocrites for the witness they bore that led to sorrowful results: "You travel over land and sea to win a single convert, and when he becomes one, you make him twice as much a son of hell as you are" (Matt. 23:15).

Help!

I don't want to learn effective witnessing techniques and then discover that my witnessing effectively led people farther away from Christ. I want the totality of my witness to bring people closer to Jesus, never away from Him. That means that it's vital for me to submit my own heart to God on a daily basis so that my witness will be pure.

Jesus said, "Apart from me you can do nothing" (John 15:5). "Neither can you bear fruit unless you remain in me. . . . If a man remains in me and I in him, he will bear much fruit" (verses 4, 5). This again highlights the importance of a consistent devotional life of study and prayer, and of a daily search for the infilling of the Holy Spirit that our witnessing might bear good fruit.

In this light I have found witnessing to have a boomerang effect. When I work and pray for the salvation of others, I sense a greater need for God in my own life. And that's the way it's supposed to happen. "If you will go to work as Christ designs that His disciples shall, and win souls for Him, you will feel the need of a deeper experience and a greater knowledge in divine things, and will hunger and thirst after righteousness. . . . Those who thus devote themselves to unselfish effort for the good of others are most surely working out their own salvation."[3]

Many have mistakenly taken refuge in their witnessing activities and success as apparent evidence that their hearts are right with God. It can be a fatal deception. Paul, the greatest missionary of them all, said, "I keep under my body, and bring it into subjection: lest that by any means, when I have preached to others, I myself should be a castaway" (1 Cor. 9:27, KJV).

2. Pray for God to give you someone you can influence for Christ. Start offering that prayer and keep on praying it until you are certain God has answered it.

God may open your eyes to someone close to home, perhaps

even *within* your home, whose heart He has prepared for your spiritual influence. He may lead you to someone you work with. Or He may work miraculously to team you up with someone you have never met before, as He introduced Philip to the Ethiopian (Acts 8), and guided Peter to the home of the Roman centurion (Acts 10). During your daily devotional time pray for spiritual discernment that you might recognize the one God guides you to.

If God does not seem to answer your prayer right away, do not panic and dart ahead of Him. Allow Him the freedom to work according to His own timetable. Continue to prepare your own heart through a consistent devotional life, and be faithful in whatever duty lies before you. God will answer your prayer in His own time and way, and in a way that you will recognize.

When God does direct you to someone, stay by that person as long as he or she gives evidence of a willingness to continue growing in Christ and Christian discipleship.

3. Get your heart into a nonjudgmental frame. In chapter 7, "How to Go to Church With Someone You Don't Agree With," I discussed the freedom Jesus gave you to accept fellow members as being as sincere in their relationship with God as you are seeking to be in yours. It is important to make that same application to anyone God might lead you to influence for Him. We are not the all-wise teachers of the ignorant, but fellow pilgrims learning His way together.

Make it a policy to never tear down someone else's religion. If you want to win others, don't bulldoze down the shanty spiritual edifice they've sought shelter in, but build a beautiful palace alongside it and invite them to move in.

Jesus said: "Do not give dogs what is sacred; do not throw your pearls to pigs. If you do, they may trample them under their feet, and then turn and tear you to pieces" (Matt. 7:6). I believe that, in part, this means that if you consider others to be inferior to you (as the Jews considered the Samaritans to be like dogs and pigs), they will detect your condescending attitude and reject anything you try to share with them. If you do not respect and love them as the children of God, then do not try to share your pearls of truth with them until you do, or they will reject them.

I had two experiences several years ago that drove this truth home to me. The first took place in the church foyer. A nurse we had baptized brought Rick, one of her patients, to church. Rick was different from the rest of us. He was a quadriplegic. I saw immediately that the greeters were not sure what to do. Unable to shake hands, he could hold his head up only a few seconds before it would fall down on his chest again with a thud. Spittle drooled from the side of his mouth and down onto his shirt. To talk, Rick had to take a deep breath and then cough out his words, which even then came out garbled and hard to understand. We were a very friendly church and tried to be polite, but we just didn't know how to really connect with him. I don't think anyone meant to look down on him, but I sensed that Rick felt very much out of place there. I'll never forget the fearful look on his face. During the week I visited him, but he didn't seem particularly interested in further contact with us.

The other incident involved Jim, who had taken his monthly check to a local bar. Two days later he still hadn't come home, leaving his wife, Ann, who was one of our members, and their two children without food. It wasn't the first time this had happened. We had helped Ann several times before when she was in a similar situation. This time I decided to go to the tavern myself and try to retrieve Jim and admonish him again concerning his responsibility to his family. When I entered the tavern I saw Jim with another woman. Taking a seat at another table, I watched them. Jim and I were in the process of trading stares when the door to the tavern opened. I probably wouldn't have even noticed, except that nearly half the people there ran over and gathered around their new guest, showering him with hearty welcomes. For just a brief moment the crowd parted, and I caught a brief glimpse of the celebrated entrant. I spotted the spittle drooling from his mouth down onto his shirt. Then the crowd closed around him again, hugging and stroking him, getting spital all over themselves. Then I heard his head go thud on his chest. The crowd parted again, and I'll never forget the look I saw on Rick's face. It was beaming. They accepted Rick, and he knew it.

At first I thought, *Well sure, when people drink they lose their sense of judgment and get friendlier.* That seemed to help for a while. But eventually Ephesians 5:18 eroded my self-justification: "Do not get drunk on wine. . . . Instead, be filled with the Spirit." How would we have received Rick at our church if we had been filled with the Spirit?

In the Winter Quarter 1983 issue of *Leadership,* Charles

Swindoll quotes the following: "The neighborhood bar is possibly the best counterfeit that there is to the fellowship Christ wants to give His church. It's an imitation, dispensing liquor instead of grace, escape rather than reality—but it is a permissive, accepting, and inclusive fellowship. It is unshockable. It is democratic. You can tell people secrets, and they usually don't tell others or even want to. The bar flourishes not because most people are alcoholics, but because God has put into the human heart the desire to know and to be known, to love and be loved, and so many seek a counterfeit at the price of a few beers. With all my heart I believe that Christ wants His church to be unshockable, a fellowship in which people can come in and say, 'I'm sunk, I'm beat, I've had it.' Alcoholics Anonymous has this quality—our churches too often miss it."

The old adage still holds true: People don't care how much you know until they know how much you care.

4. Take advantage of the power of your personal testimony. Modern marketers have discovered the age-old principle that products are most effectively promoted through personal testimonies— Nikes (Michael Jordan), Diet Pepsi (Ray Charles), Equal (Cher), etc. Revelation 12:11 reveals that Satan is overcome in people's lives by the blood of the Lamb and the word of their testimony. It seems to me that many Adventists do not realize the power that their personal testimonies can have in the lives of those they seek to win to Christ and the church.

The Four Elements of a Winning Personal Testimony

Element One: Be aware of the great things God has done for you. Mary confessed, "The Mighty One has done great things for me—holy is his name" (Luke 1:49). Can you make that same confession? Are you aware of the wonderful things that God has done for you? Such an awareness is the foundation of your testimony.

Element Two: Treasure those things in your heart. As she contemplated the miraculous events surrounding the birth of Jesus, "Mary treasured up all these things and pondered them in her heart" (Luke 2:19). It's easy to forget the great things God has done for us, or to take them for granted. But to have a winning personal testimony we must fix them in our memory.

Element Three: Share with others the great things God has

done for you. Luke relates the well-known story of the demon-pos-sessed man whom Jesus healed. The frightened villagers asked Jesus to leave. "The man from whom the demons had gone out begged to go with him, but Jesus sent him away, saying, 'Return home and tell how much God has done for you.' So the man went away and told all over town how much Jesus had done for him" (Luke 8:38, 39).

Having never taken a series of Bible studies himself, he knew nothing about how to give them to others. He may not even have ever read the Bible. Yet Jesus sent him back to his village, armed with the one thing he knew—he had been healed. That was his tes-timony, the story of what God had done for him. And that story en-abled him to be a mighty witness for God.

Following Matthew's account of this story that identifies two demon-possessed men, Ellen White noted: "They could not instruct the people as the disciples who had been daily with Christ were able to do. But they bore in their own persons the evidence that Jesus was the Messiah. They could tell what they knew; what they them-selves had seen, and heard, and felt of the power of Christ. This is what everyone can do whose heart has been touched by the grace of God. . . . This is the witness for which our Lord calls, and for want of which the world is perishing."[4]

Ellen White repeatedly emphasizes the importance of personal testimony: "We are to acknowledge His grace as made known through the holy men of old; but that which will be most effectual is the testimony of our own experience."[5] In other words, we should teach people about the Bible, but "the testimony of our own expe-rience" is an even more effective witness.

"These precious acknowledgments to the praise of the glory of His grace, when supported by a Christlike life, have an irresistible power that works for the salvation of souls."[6] We know, of course, that an "irresistible" testimony can be resisted, else the many pleas of the loyal angels would have prevented Lucifer from ever leaving heaven. But the point is made clear enough—your personal testi-mony of the great things God has done for you is a powerfully per-suasive witness for God.

Element Four: Our testimonies should not point people to ourselves, but we should use our stories to point people to Jesus. A Samaritan woman with a bad reputation had a life-changing encounter with Jesus. As she shared that experience with her towns-people, her story became an "irresistible" testimony through the power of the Holy Spirit. At first, "many of the Samaritans from that town believed in him because of the woman's testimony" (John. 4:39). But what she said led her friends to listen to Jesus for themselves. "And because of his words many more became believ-ers. They said to the woman, 'We no longer believe just because of what you said; now we have heard for ourselves, and we know that this man really is the Savior of the world' " (verses 41, 42).

As He did with the demon-possessed men and the woman of Samaria, the Holy Spirit can use your testimony as "an irresistible power" to reach hearts that will not listen to Jesus any other way.

5. Get a set of Bible lessons that you can go through with those interests God leads you to. I've heard some members criti-cize this approach as too mechanical, but 25 years of experience has taught me the wisdom of using a set of Bible lessons as the basis for working with people God leads me to influence for Him. Such an approach avoids the Columbus syndrome: When Columbus started out on his famous voyage, he didn't know where he was going; when he got there, he didn't know where he was; and when he got back home, he didn't know where he'd been. The same can be true in working with a spiritual interest unless you have some sort of map to guide you. A good set of Bible lessons can be an invaluable map by which to chart your course.

I've heard the objection that most printed lessons available today are too legalistic in their orientation. But even if that were true, I've learned that the Christian experience of the lesson-giver is far more important than the printed text of the lessons themselves in terms of communicating a proper orientation to the gospel.

Your local Adventist Book Center has a number of good Bible study courses available. The Good News for Today lessons, written by Don and Marge Gray, are conveniently paginated to a special paperback edition of The New King James Version. Hart Research has produced a series entitled "Come Alive/Stay Alive," designed especially for those with little or no Bible background, but it lacks the coordinated pagination that makes it easier for some people to find their way around in the Bible.

My experience has taught me to use the lessons just as they are, simply and with little embellishment except as the person I'm working with asks questions. Also I share my personal testimony as it relates to each lesson—sometimes sharing an experience I have had in my life related to one of the points made in the lesson, at other times simply by expressing how much one of the texts referred to in the lesson has meant to me.

Most conferences have some kind of training program to help you learn how to use such lessons. But the best way is just to go through them with as many people as God leads you to who have an interest in such a study. You can even ask a friend to study the lessons with you as practice sessions. It's helpful the first time through to accompany a pastor or lay Bible worker and observe how they do it. It's also valuable to team up with someone else when giving Bible studies, but with the understanding that only one person leads out for each study.

To get a Bible study started, simply ask the person you believe God has led you to if he or she might have an interest in studying the Bible in a systematic way through a series of lessons that cover its major themes. If they decline your invitation it's a sign that they aren't ready yet. Sometimes they will be more receptive to such studies later on in your friendship.

Several months ago I began praying for another person to work with. Shortly thereafter, my wife's friend mentioned that her non-Adventist husband, Brad, seemed to be becoming more receptive to spiritual things. So we went out to dinner together at a nice restaurant and socialized for the evening. When we returned to his house I commented that I had seen him in church and appreciated his visit. When he responded by telling me that he had enjoyed the church service, that opened the door for me to proceed further. I told him about a series of lessons that I thought he might be interested in that give an orientation to the major themes of the Bible in a systematic way. When he told me that the lessons sounded interesting to him, he opened another door for me, so I told him that I could come by the next Tuesday evening and show him one of the lessons and explain how they worked. We made the appointment, and the studies were underway. Recently he and his sister were baptized, and they are now trying to involve other family members in a similar study program. It doesn't always work that smoothly, and you will encounter many valid variations on the theme, but it never hurts to ask people if they might be interested in studying Scripture.

6. Pray for the spiritual welfare of the people you are studying with, asking God to work signs and wonders, if need be, to secure them for His kingdom. The beleaguered disciples of Jesus prayed: "Enable your servants to speak your word with great boldness. Stretch out your hand to heal and perform miraculous signs and wonders through the name of your holy servant Jesus" (Acts 4:29, 30). We modern disciples of Jesus ought not to be afraid to pray with equal boldness.

I once studied with a family that went beyond my ability to help. Mary had attended Sabbath school several times with Lisa, her 5-year-old daughter, and Bruce, her 3-year-old son. The kindergarten leader pointed them out to me, so I visited this family and offered to go through a set of Bible lessons with Mary and David, her husband. We were only about five lessons into the series when Mary began pressing me about the Adventist position on jewelry. She had noticed that the women in our church wore very little jewelry, and wondered if that was a church teaching. Although I tried to stay with the subject of the lesson, she was insistent. After sharing a couple texts that identified the principle of inward adornment, I then returned to the lesson.

The next week when Mary answered her door, she looked like the decked-out woman of Revelation 17—rings on *every* finger, heavy make-up, necklaces, and bracelets. She informed me that her inheritance was in jewelry, and that most of her jewelry had been in her family for years. Our study that evening was on God and His love for us. At the end of the study Mary said that she didn't believe God loved her and wasn't even sure He existed. Before I left that night, I prayed a very bold prayer, asking God to reveal His love to Mary in some way that she couldn't deny.

The next day I was taking phone messages off my office answering machine when I heard an out-of-breath voice exclaiming, "This is Mary Dunbar. This is Mary Dunbar. I know that God loves me. I know that God loves me." Needless to say, I was both thankful and curious. When I returned her call, she told me this story.

That morning she had invited her neighbor and children to go shopping with her. On the way to the mall Mary had complained about the "unbiblical" rules and regulations that the Adventists had, about how she could never in a million years become a member of such a church, how she wasn't sure there was a God, and even if one did exist, He didn't love her.

After she had been at the mall about an hour, she noticed that little Bruce was missing, her clingy child who never let Mommy out of his sight. She hurried back through the aisles of the store she was in. No Bruce. Now she began retracing her steps through other stores she had been in, but no one could even remember seeing a 3-year-old boy matching Bruce's description.

Finally Mary realized that Bruce was lost. At that point she panicked and became one of the proverbial fox-hole Christians. Ordinarily she was so self-conscious about her own spirituality that she wouldn't even say a prayer with her children before they ate a meal. But with Bruce gone nothing else mattered anymore. She knelt down in the middle of the mall, with people going by her on both sides, and cried out to God that her child was lost and she had to find him. No sooner had these words gone out of her mouth than something like a voice spoke to her consciousness like a thunderbolt, "No, Mary, you are the child who is lost, My lost child whom I love and am trying to reclaim."

It took Mary another 20 minutes to find Bruce, who had climbed behind some long coats in the women's department and had fallen asleep. But Mary's life had changed. From that day forward I never saw a piece of jewelry on her. Nor do I remember that the subject ever came up again. She and David were baptized several months later.

Here again, God doesn't always answer our prayers for miracles. At the moment I am working with a man who needs to quit smoking. I prayed with him that God would perform a miracle to completely remove his desire to smoke. Unfortunately he is still addicted to the habit. But he still continues to come to church and show an openness to spiritual things. So I will continue to pray and work with him for as long as it takes.

But even in those cases where God does not answer my prayer with an obvious miracle, I believe it is still appropriate to ask for His direct divine intervention on behalf of those He has led us to.

I have also had to face the harsh reality that God Himself has to deal with constantly—not all who hear His call will accept Jesus and choose to be saved.

7. Keep in touch with your pastor, informing him or her of the progress that your witnessing is making. Your pastor may be eager to pray for your interest, may be able to provide you with valuable counsel along the way, would likely be willing to make a timely visit now and then if you feel it would augment your own ministry to the person, and may be especially helpful when the individual is ready to make a decision for Christ or church membership.

Witness Through Daily Life

I have found these seven principles of witnessing to be very powerful when applied. But they are not a mechanical formula that allows no deviation, nor do I suggest that there is only one way to witness effectively. "The greater part of our Saviour's life on earth was spent in patient toil in the carpenter's shop at Nazareth. Ministering angels attended the Lord of life as He walked side by side with peasants and laborers, unrecognized and unhonored. He was as faithfully fulfilling His mission while working at His humble trade as when He healed the sick or walked upon the storm-tossed waves of Galilee. So in the humblest duties and lowliest positions of life, we may walk and work with Jesus. . . .

"The businessman may conduct his business in a way that will glorify his Master because of his fidelity. . . . The mechanic may be a diligent and faithful representative of Him who toiled in the lowly walks of life among the hills of Galilee. . . .

"If your daily life is a testimony to the purity and sincerity of your faith, and others are convinced that you desire to benefit them, your efforts will not be wholly lost.

"The humblest and poorest of the disciples of Jesus can be a blessing to others. They may not realize that they are doing any special good, but by their unconscious influence they may start waves of blessing that will widen and deepen, and the blessed results they may never know until the day of final reward. They do not feel or know that they are doing anything great. They are not required to weary themselves with anxiety about success. They have only to go forward quietly, doing faithfully the work that God's providence assigns, and their life will not be in vain."[7]

In chapter 1 I told the story of how my son Andrew woke up in the middle of the night on a backpacking trip, screaming in terror, and how his fear instantly melted into peace when I shined the flashlight so that he could see my face. That is how I see my role as a witness for God and Jesus, to let my life and testimony and witness be the beam of light that shows the Father's face. That face can bring peace to every heart that beholds it and learns to know its trustworthy love.

The Eternal Reward

God has assured Ordinary Adventists who are faithful to their calling to be His witnesses of an incredible reunion in heaven one day: "The redeemed will meet and recognize those whose attention they have directed to the uplifted Saviour. What blessed converse they have with these souls! 'I was a sinner,' it will be said, 'without God and without hope in the world, and you came to me and drew my attention to the precious Saviour as my only hope.'. . .

"Others will express their gratitude to those who fed the hungry and clothed the naked. 'When despair bound my soul in unbelief, the Lord sent you to me,' they say, 'to speak words of hope and comfort. You brought me food for my physical necessities, and you opened to me the Word of God, awakening me to my spiritual needs. You treated me as a brother. You sympathized with me in my sorrows, and restored my bruised and wounded soul, so that I could grasp the hand of Christ that was reached out to save me. In my ignorance you taught me patiently that I had a Father in heaven who cared for me. You read to me the precious promises of God's Word. You inspired in me the faith that He would save me. My heart was softened, subdued, broken, as I contemplated the sacrifice which Christ had made for me. . . . I am here, saved, eternally saved, ever to live in His presence and to praise Him who gave His life for me.'"[8]

---

[1] E. G. White, *The Ministry of Healing,* p. 143.

[2] ———— , *Steps to Christ,* p. 78.

[3] *Ibid.,* p. 80.

[4] ———— , *The Desire of Ages,* p. 340.

[5] *Ibid.,* p. 347.

[6] *Ibid.*

[7] ———— , *Steps to Christ,* pp. 81-83.

[8] ———— , *Maranatha: The Lord Is Coming* (Washington, D.C.: Review and Herald Pub. Assn., 1976), p. 303.

LOOKING THROUGH HIS EYES

MERCY

BLESS

kindness

forgive

CHAPTER 15

Those Extraordinary Ordinaries

In her two excellent books, *Paint the World With Love* and *Paint the World With Love, Second Coat,* Jeannette Johnson highlights stories of "ordinary Adventists doing extraordinary things to change their corner of the world." In so doing, she skillfully presented the point that I felt needed to be made in conclusion—ordinary Adventists are often anything but ordinary.

The July 1990 edition of the *Signs of the Times* was a special edition entitled "Portraits of a People." It featured Seventh-day Adventists who have received recognition for the high levels of excellence they have achieved in their specialized professions. Spotlight: Harry Anderson, "the foremost illustrator of religious subjects in the twentieth century." Spotlight: Dr. Ben Carson, who went from childhood in an impoverished neighborhood in Detroit to become the director of the Division of Pediatric Neurosurgery at Johns Hopkins University and Hospital. Spotlight: Desmond Doss, the only soldier in World War II to receive the Congressional Medal of Honor without ever having fired a shot. Spotlight: Chessie Harris, awarded the Volunteer Action Award by President George Bush for finding homes (her own included) for more than 900 foster children, many of whom matured into successful adults.

The editors designed this special issue of *Signs* to be distributed throughout Indianapolis just prior to the 1990 General Conference session. When the church wanted to let that great city know what Seventh-day Adventists are about, it wisely chose to spotlight its members as well as its beliefs.

I felt a wholesome pride as I read the reports of these extraordinary Adventists. But I also greatly appreciated the introductory remarks then-editor Kenneth Holland made to the special issue: "I know of people, fellow believers, whom I don't wish to identify in any way, whose lives of sacrifice and faith simply astound me and inspire me. They are among people with plain faces you would never note—with ineloquent words you'd never quote—whose dreams for themselves are ever postponed by the needs or wants of their spouses, then their children, then their spouses again. These make a difference in our world too."

I too have been simply astounded and inspired by the lives of many ordinary Adventists in the congregations I have pastored. I believe they are one of Jesus' greatest gifts to us as a people. He enlightens our understanding so that we might see His glory shining through the unassuming deeds of even the least and humblest of our fellow members. "From now on," as Paul said, "we regard no one from a human point of view" (2 Cor. 5:16, NRSV).

In Hebrews 11 God recognized some of His heroes of old— from Abel to Moses, and "the prostitute Rahab, because she welcomed the spies" (verse 31). At the end of this list, the author thinks of the many less well-known, but no less glorious heroes and laments that he doesn't have the time to recognize them all: "And what more shall I say? I do not have time to tell about Gideon, Barak, Samson, Jephthah, . . ." etc., including "women" who "received back their dead, raised to life again" (verses 32, 35). Isn't that just like real life today? We don't have time to recognize the noble deeds regularly being performed all around us. But I have found that to the extent that I take the time to recognize them, it enriches me.

• • •

When it came time for the church to choose the head elder for the new year, it was only natural that they asked Ron, a medical doctor whose consistent Christian life had been recognized by the congregation he served as an elder for the previous several years, and as head elder for the year just ending. But when asked to be the head elder again, Ron disclosed that after reevaluating his own spiritual gifts, he felt he could better serve the church in some position that required attention to small details. We did need someone to serve as personal ministries and Sabbath school secretary, a position that demanded attention to details. Ron gladly accepted those positions and performed an excellent ministry for the church through them. Many would have been too proud to go from head elder to Sabbath school secretary, but for Ron it was an honor because he felt he could use his spiritual gifts most beneficially for the church in that kind of ministry.

• • •

The church is filled with unrecognized heroes, extraordinary ordinaries, whose unobtrusive acts of kindness and mercy bring delight to the heart of their Father. Jesus, through David, testified of them: "As for the saints who are in the land, they are the glorious ones in whom is all my delight" (Ps. 16:3). Zephaniah assures those who seek humbly to bless others and glorify God through the little acts of daily life, "The Lord your God is with you, he is mighty to save. He will take great delight in you, he will quiet you with his love, he will rejoice over you with singing" (Zeph. 3:17).

When you walk into your church next Sabbath, take the time to look around at your fellow members. Can you sense the awesomeness of being in the presence of those who are the delight of Jesus, and over whom the Father sings with rejoicing? Serving in the Sabbath school divisions, sitting in the pews, and functioning on the platform are people whose stories and lives bear the imprint of God's living power and grace. Allow yourself to be inspired and astounded Sabbath after Sabbath by God's gift as reflected in these "ordinary" people who touch other lives profoundly in small and unobtrusive ways, without fanfare or acclaim.

• • •

I first met Matt at a seminar we conducted entitled "How to Know God." He was the lead guitarist in a local rock band. But during our seminar Matt found a new love. His subsequent life as an Adventist Christian was not without its intense struggles, but his very presence in our congregation testified to the mighty power of God. During prayer request time at prayer meeting one evening, Matt raised his hand and reported that someone had stolen his motorcycle that very day. "Let's pray that Matt's motorcycle will be found," I interrupted. But he corrected me, "No, Pastor, I've committed all my possessions to God, and it's all right for Him to do what He chooses with His own property. My concern is for the person who stole my motorcycle. He must not know Jesus as I now have the joy of knowing Him. I would like us to pray that this person will come to know the freedom that Jesus gives us to love Him more than our possessions."

• • •

Jesus Himself said that a prophet is without honor "in his own country" (Matt. 13:57, KJV). It's true, isn't it? The closer we live to each other, the easier it is to see each other's warts and ineptitudes. We know each other to be "recovering sinners," and the more we know each other, the easier it is to recognize the validity of the "sinner" portion of that label, and to overlook the little evidences along the way that recovery is indeed in progress. Parents who live with their children day by day don't notice how fast they're growing as easily as visiting relatives do who haven't seen the youngsters for a while. The same thing happens in the church. It's hard to notice how far sinners have grown toward spiritual heroism when you sit down the pew from them week after week. But it's so easy to miss the many ways God is being glorified through the little acts of courtesy and thoughtfulness of brothers and sisters in our churches whom we have grown to know well. A prophet is, indeed, without honor in his own country.

God offers to remove the scales from our eyes. He extends to us the Spirit's eyesalve that enables us to "regard no one from a human point of view." Once you become sensitized to such recognition, then it can happen anytime. You can be having a routine encounter with a fellow member, and suddenly a wonderful revelation takes place in which you see the glory of God shining as bright as noonday.

• • •

It had been about five years since Lorrell had come back to the church. In his quiet way he had gained the confidence of many in our congregation and had accepted the nominating committee's request to serve as one of our elders. I was picking him up at the local Ford dealer where he worked so we could go to lunch together.

While waiting for him, I visited with the manager of the shop, who praised the quality and efficiency of Lorrell's work. I proceeded to Lorrell's bay to see how much longer he would be. He was underneath the front end of the car, operating a power sander. Bending down, I observed that he was persistently trying to smooth out an almost minuscule indentation that lodged a tiny fleck of rust. When I later inquired why he worked so hard on a spot that no one would probably ever notice, he answered, "Before any car leaves my bay, I like to have it ready for Jesus to drive."

• • •

Once we acquire eyes to see the glory of God reflected in the lives of fellow members, the next step is to learn to express our appreciation to them for the blessing they are to us. Such a suggestion draws us into murky waters because of the counsel we have received against flattering people. But flattery is insincere praise given for some ulterior motive. There is a way to express appreciation for blessings that encourages and strengthens, rather than harms, the recipient.

People criticized Mary for spending a year's wages on perfume that she poured on Jesus in a single act. Her critics accused her of uselessly squandering money that could have gone to the poor. But Jesus defended her for appreciating Him with her gift of love. "And as He went down into the darkness of His great trial, He carried with Him the memory of that deed, an earnest of the love that would be His from His redeemed ones forever."[1]

Drawing from Mary's lavish expression of appreciation for Christ, Ellen White drew this practical lesson: "Many there are who bring their precious gifts for the dead. As they stand about the cold, silent form, words of love are freely spoken. Tenderness, appreciation, devotion, all are lavished upon one who sees not nor hears. Had these words been spoken when the weary spirit needed them so much, when the ear could hear and the heart could feel, how precious would have been their fragrance!"[2]

• • •

Wendy has a special gift. Knowing how to bless people with words of encouragement and appreciation, she has an uncanny ability to sense when someone is having a struggle of some kind. If they don't get a reassuring word from her in church, they're likely to get a note in the mail. As I've made pastoral visits I've noticed personalized scriptures on cards from Wendy taped to refrigerator doors in numerous homes. Little streams of light imperceptibly beaming into the lives of others through one of God's special children.

• • •

Everyone with whom we live and worship who will ultimately be saved will one day be a great celebrity. Paul revealed this in one of his most exalted revelations that envisioned the afterlife as though it were already a present reality: "And God raised us up with Christ and seated us with him in the heavenly realms in Christ Jesus, in order that in the coming ages he might show the incomparable riches of his grace, expressed in his kindness to us in Christ Jesus" (Eph. 2:6, 7).

In these verses Paul presents the redeemed as though they've already been raised from the dead and are seated with Jesus in heaven. But his portrayal doesn't stop there. He doesn't leave us with a picture of saved people statically sitting alongside Jesus forever. Instead He pictures them with full calendars of guest-speaking appointments on planet after planet, receiving the red-carpet treatment from various life-forms who dwell in every portion of the universe, all of whom have the greatest respect and admiration for the redeemed children from Planet Earth. And why are they such sought-after guest speakers? Because every one of them has a story to tell that the inhabitants of the universe long to hear over and over again, a story that will "show the incomparable riches of his grace, expressed in his kindness to us in Christ Jesus." "Tell us," they will say, "of the mighty things that God did for you. Tell us how you were introduced to Jesus when you lived on earth. Tell us what it was like to commune with Him each day even though you couldn't see Him. Tell us how you overcame your doubts and fears. Tell us about your prayers, those that were clearly answered and those that didn't seem to be. We want to hear about them all. Tell us how God helped you through the trials and discouragements of your life. Tell us how you prayed and worked that others might be here. Tell us of the greatest joys you had. Tell us how Satan, whom we once knew as our brother Lucifer, was finally overcome in your life. Tell us everything about it. Please tell it all." The testimonies that mean so much to us and others here will mean as much or more to them. And we will never tire of telling the story of how in so many practical ways and through so many special people He showed to us the incomparable riches of His grace expressed in His kindness to us in Christ Jesus.

• • •

"Pastor, if I have to forgive that woman to get to heaven, then I know I'm not going. I could never forgive her for what she did to my son." I understood the strength of Sadie's feelings. Several years earlier her son, Daniel, had gone through a difficult period in his marriage. Sensing his vulnerability, another woman moved in, causing Daniel to lose his marriage and become estranged from his children. The incident still hurt Sadie. "Now I can't even see my own grandchildren. I hate that woman." But over a period of months I saw a beautiful healing come into Sadie's heart. She reconciled to Debbie, the woman she had so hated. After Debbie's marriage to Daniel, Sadie even allowed them to move into her home for a few months during a critical time when Daniel was between jobs. There's nothing about Sadie that would particularly cause the world to take note of her. But as I saw mother and daughter-in-law attending church together, the bonds of friendship growing between them, I thought I could hear the choirs of heaven bursting forth in magnificent praise to God. I thank God for allowing me to witness His miracle of grace in that humble earthen vessel. Her example has called my own heart to greater spiritual heights. Sadie's story deserves to be retold again and again through the ages.

• • •

Those today who are the most inept of God's children here, the most unsophisticated, the most unattractive, the most uncouth, the most clumsy, the most awkward, will in the ages to come be refined to perfection. Their features will be stunningly attractive then, their mannerisms cultured and genteel, their words articulate and powerful. The weakest among us now will then be respected and admired as heroes.

God does not look upon His children here in the same way we are so prone to regard each other. For He is a "God who . . . calls things that are not as though they were" (Rom. 4:17). He sees them as they will be in the age to come, with the dignified bearing of kings and queens, priests of the most high God. The Lord treats them now with the honor and respect that will be their due then. At the same time He grants us the freedom to value each other with the same esteem that He does. God gives us the freedom to look past each other's faults and imperfections, the freedom to love each other as we are, the freedom to catch a vision of the restored and dignified beings we will ultimately be through Christ.

● ● ●

He hardly looked like Dr. Paul Smith anymore. Normally as small in stature as he was tall in spirit, his frail body was now bloated to twice its usual size, with tubes protruding from practically every opening in his body. His meticulous attention to God's laws of health had kept him in excellent health well into his fifty-sixth year, giving credibility to the medical practice and health education center that he operated with his brother Charles, a man of equal spiritual stature. The diagnosis of a rare type of melanoma four months earlier could hardly have been more unbelievable. As predicted, the cancer did its dastardly deed swiftly in spite of an avalanche of prayers for healing. Now he was in and out of consciousness in a small experimental hospital in southern California. His wife and six daughters pressed close to catch the sense of his every whisper. Paul's words, no longer formed by conscious intention, were the unconscious expression of the last vestiges of the spirit within him and revealed who he really was at the very core of his being. A last gasping breath prepared him for his final sounds that were more audible than his recent whispers. His last words were garbled but clearly intelligible—he was praying for his family. His soul had been purged of all earthly dross. I don't know if I believe in sinless perfection as a theological concept. He and I used to debate it. I kidded him that he couldn't reach the perfection he sought until he agreed with me more than he did. But that day I may have come as close to witnessing human perfection as I ever will again on this earth. I felt I was on holy ground as I saw him breathe his last and then relax in peace. This spiritual gladiator, who had fought a good fight and finished his course, now awaited the crown God had laid up for him.

• • •

As we continue seeking Him on a daily basis, God will enlighten our vision that we might never again regard one another from a human point of view, never again fail to be astounded and inspired by those extraordinary ordinaries.

---

[1] E. G. White, *The Desire of Ages,* p. 560.
[2] *Ibid.*

Epilogue

Once I accepted the invitation to write this book, I spent several hours drafting a covering prayer for the project. Before I would begin work on a new chapter or take up editing an already drafted one, I would bring this prayer anew to God in its entirety. I wish I could say that I did this out of a deep level of spiritual maturity. The truth of the matter is, I did it out of a keen awareness of my need as a writer.

The covering prayer for *Things We Don't Talk About* was a secret between God and me until I showed it to a couple close friends toward the completion of the manuscript. Now, after considerable prayer to God and debate within myself, I have decided to share it with you for two reasons: First, that you might have another glimpse into the private life of this ordinary Adventist, to know the motivation and intent behind every subject dealt with. But more important, because I would appreciate hearing from you if some of the requests I made relative to the reader were answered in any measure in your life as you read it.

In addition, I would like to learn more about the private life of ordinary Adventists. If you would be willing to share with me some of the inner workings of your own heart as they relate to the Adventist faith and hope, I would be pleased. Understand that I cannot provide a long-distance counseling service, nor am I qualified to do so. But listening to your experience will enrich my own and could give greater depth and

authenticity to any writing I may attempt in the future.
    You may write to: Skip MacCarty
                      c/o Pioneer Memorial SDA Church
                      400 University Blvd.
                      Berrien Springs, MI 49103
                      Fax: 616-471-6152
                      E-mail: 74532,665@compuserve.com

Prayer for
the Private Life of
an Ordinary Adventist

"Ask and it will be given to you" (Matt. 7:7).

Father, before I ever write a word on this manuscript I bring it in its entirety to You. "Except the Lord build the house, they labor in vain who build it" (Ps. 127:1, KJV). Unless You are in this manuscript from the first word to the last, I labor in vain in writing it. I would rather have it pleasing to You and that You be in it wholly, than it be a best-seller. I ask that everyone who shall ever read it will receive a personal word from their Father, a word that will be as a savor of life unto life. May it not present a low view of the Christian walk, as I am all too prone to walk myself, but a high view. And may my own life in the writing be Spirit-nourished and -enabled, drawn up into the higher life represented herein.

1. Cleanse my heart and mind and life to correspond to the noble themes You may draw me to.

2. Grant me a heart and spirit that will hear the still small voice of Your Spirit guiding in insight, thought, and language.

3. Grant me efficiency in the writing. I do not ask to be delivered from the discipline of a writer. Instead I ask only that I might be prevented from wandering the long, tedious trails of thought that lead nowhere and consume enormous amounts of time to no fruitful end. I would love to be able to write quickly and with sterling quality.

4. Grant me a persevering spirit that will not give up no matter how discouraged I may feel somewhere along the way.

5. Turn me quickly from this project if it would not glorify You. I accept the invitation, twice extended, from the Review as an opportunity granted by You to share in wider circles some of what You have taught me.

6. Protect me and my family from the harm Satan may seek to bring upon us during this period of writing.

7. Help me be brief and to the point. Economy of words. The less-is-more principle. Yet depth and breadth of thought and experience. And a length acceptable to the editors.

8. May Your heart shine forth on every page. May no one read any length at all without knowing for certain to the very depth of their being that God deeply loves them. May they sense the attractiveness of Your character and be drawn to Your heart thereby.

9. Help me to portray the gospel with integrity. May I not water it down. May its radical call to wholehearted, uncompromising discipleship ring with crystal clarity. And may I be able to say with Paul: "My way of life in Christ Jesus . . . agrees with what I teach" (1 Cor. 4:17).

10. May this book lead to conversions and reconversions to Jesus Christ. May readers come into deeper love of God through their reading. May they be drawn by the compelling power of Your love deeper into the Christian walk. May they come to rest in Your love, rest completely, securely, and joyfully with a faith that works by love.